Be a Work of Art: 250 Anecdotes and Stories

David Bruce

Published by David Bruce, 2022.

While every precaution has been taken in the preparation of this book, the publisher assumes no responsibility for errors or omissions, or for damages resulting from the use of the information contained herein.

BE A WORK OF ART: 250 ANECDOTES AND STORIES

First edition. December 27, 2022.

Copyright © 2022 David Bruce.

ISBN: 979-8215604182

Written by David Bruce.

Table of Contents

Dedication

Dedicated to My Uncle Reuben Saturday

When he was a young man, my mother's brother Reuben wanted to escape from poverty and lard sandwiches, so he tried to run away from it. He stole a car so he could drive up north where he hoped to find opportunity, but he got caught and ended up on a Georgia chain gang for several months. In a chain gang, prisoners are shackled every few feet by the ankles to a long length of chain to keep them from escaping. They work in the hot sun while shackled to the chain, and when they sleep, they are shackled to the bed. No freedom, hard work, hot sun, no pay, bad food, and some mean guards.

When my uncle got released from the chain gang, he hitchhiked up north. He did what a lot of people trying to escape from poverty do: He drifted. He drifted from town to town, seeking opportunity and not finding it. He worked when he could, but the jobs were temporary and low pay. My uncle slept rough often, and he was hungry often. Once, when he was completely broke and completely hungry, he saw a restaurant with a buffet and went inside and asked to speak to the manager. He said, "I am very hungry, I don't have any money, and I would appreciate it very much if you would give me any food that the restaurant is going to throw away. I will be happy to wait by the rear entrance until you are ready to throw away food."

The manager told him to sit down at a table, and then the manager went to the buffet, loaded a big plate high with food, and gave it to him free of charge.

One way out of poverty is to get a good job, and my uncle got out of poverty by getting a job working with sheet metal.

My uncle's work ethic helped him. His employer sent him to California to do some special sheet-metal work, and the people in California wanted to keep him there. They explained that their

California employees liked to come to work late, leave early, and take many days off. It was difficult to get someone who would show up and do the work they were supposed to do and were paid to do.

My uncle was also good with money. He got married, bought a house, and raised six children. Each time he made a mortgage payment, he paid extra money so he could pay off the mortgage faster.

If there was a sale on food, he bought lots of it. For example, if there was a sale on peanut butter, two jars for the price of one, he would buy twelve jars and sometimes go back the next day and buy six more jars.

If you went in his pantry — a closet set aside to store food — you saw that it was packed with food. If you went in his kitchen, you saw that he had taken off the doors of the high cabinets in which he stored food so that he could see the food. If you went in his bedroom, you saw that he had all the regular bedroom furniture, but he also had lots of shelves he had installed. The shelves were loaded with things that he had bought on sale that he knew his family could use: food (of course), light bulbs, toothpaste, toilet paper, etc. His bedroom looked like a warehouse.

Once he made a bad purchase: he bought a case of baked beans. Beans are beans, but the sauce they came in can taste good or bad, and the sauce these beans came in tasted bad. His kids told him, "Dad, throw those beans away! They're awful!"

But when you grow up poor, you don't throw beans away. For a long time, whenever my uncle and his family ate baked beans, they ate a mixture of one can of good baked beans and one can of bad baked beans.

My uncle's kids never had to eat lard sandwiches.

***

The doing of good deeds is important. As a free person, you can choose to live your life as a good person or as a bad person. To be a good person, do good deeds. To be a bad person, do bad deeds.

If you do good deeds, you will become good. If you do bad deeds, you will become bad. To become the person you want to be, act as if you already are that kind of person. Each of us chooses what kind of person we will become. To become a good person, do the things a good person does. To become a bad person, do the things a bad person does. The opportunity to take action to become the kind of person you want to be is yours.

Cover Photo for *Be a Work of Art: 250 Anecdotes and Stories*: https://pixabay.com/illustrations/ballerina-swan-lake-performance-4365601/

***

Most of these anecdotes are meant to be funny, but some are meant to be thought-provoking.

***

Educate Yourself
    Read Like A Wolf Eats
    Be Excellent to Each Other
    Books Then, Books Now, Books Forever

***

Do you know a language other than English? If you do, I give you permission to translate this book, copyright your translation, publish or self-publish it, and keep all the royalties for yourself. (Do give me credit, of course, for the original book.)

Introduction

Living works of art tend to take joy in living. So how can we be a living work of art? Some ways include living a life of wit and intelligence, practicing an art, doing good deeds, paying attention to your soul as well as your body, and being aware of the fabulous realities that surround us despite the presence of evil in the world. Here are some bumper-sticker condensations of ancient and modern wisdom: Resist Psychic Death, Do It Yourself, Resist Mindless Consumption, Don't Fear the Reaper, Maintain Maximum Cool, Do Good Now (and Maybe be a Hero), Love and Live Life, Reality is Fabulous, and Vote for Women's Rights. Of course, more good advice is this: Dress Like a Work of Art.

Chapter 1: From Acting and Actors to Class

Acting and Actors

• Some people can't distinguish the actor from the actor's role. A grocer from Lichfield once carried a letter to the famous actor David Garrick from his brother. However, the grocer never delivered the letter. After seeing Mr. Garrick perform on stage the comic role of Abel Drugger in *The Alchemist* by Ben Jonson, the grocer said that he didn't want anything to do with such a shabby creature as he had seen on stage.[1]

• Sir Henry Irving (1838-1905) was proud of his performances as the lead of Shakespeare's *Macbeth*. Once he asked his dresser, Walter Collinson, to say in which play he was at his best, and he was pleased when Mr. Collinson answered, "*Macbeth*." Sir Henry said, "It is generally conceded to be *Hamlet*," but Mr. Collinson insisted, "Oh, no, Sir. *Macbeth*. You sweat twice as much in that."[2]

• In 1642, the Puritans closed the theaters in England. By the time they reopened 18 years later, the boy actors who had played the roles of women had grown up and no apprentices had been available to learn to take their places. When theater-friendly King Charles II wanted to see a play, he was forced to wait until the man playing the Queen had finished shaving.[3]

• Sam Mendes was very young — 23 years old — when he directed Judi Dench in three plays. During a conversation, they talked about some plays that Ms. Dench had starred in during the mid-1970s. Ms. Dench asked Mr. Mendes if he seen the plays, and he replied, "Well, no. I was 10 years old." Ms. Dench screamed and then pretended to choke him.[4]

• Early in his career, actor David Niven received a bad review for his performance in the movie *Dodsworth*. He had the review framed and hung it in his bathroom: "In this picture we are privileged to see Mr. Samuel Goldwyn's latest 'discovery.' All we can say about this actor is that he is tall, dark and not the slightest bit handsome."[5]

• Actress Ellen Terry once dumped the contents of her heavily filled pocketbook onto a table as she searched for a note she wanted to give to Harry Fiske. Mr. Fiske surveyed the contents of the purse and then asked, "No slingshot?" Ms. Terry replied, "No slingshot."[6]

• An actor in *Nude with A Violin* asked the playwright, Noël Coward, about the motivation of his character. Mr. Coward replied, "My dear boy, forget about the motivation. Just say the lines and don't trip over the furniture."[7]

Activism

• In 2011, the Occupy Wall Street protest against corporate greed took off and Occupy protests spread around the United States. One remarkable photo that came out of the protests is that of a woman and three dogs standing in the deserted tundra of Alaska. The woman is holding a hand-lettered cardboard sign that has this message: "Occupy the Tundra." The woman is Diane McEachern, a resident of Bethel, Alaska, a town of 6,400 people and one main street. Ms. McEachern, an assistant professor in the rural human service program at the Kuskokwim campus of the University of Alaska, posted the photograph on the Occupy Wall Street Facebook page with this caption: "I am a woman. The dogs are rescues. The tundra is outside of Bethel, Alaska. The day is chill. The sentiment is solid. Find your spot. Occupy it. Even if it is only your own mind." The photo went viral. Ms. McEachern said about the protests, "When I saw that it was growing and there was Occupying Portland and Occupying New Hampshire, I thought, for goodness' sake, what can I occupy? How can I get in on this? And I thought, well, what's my context? What's important to me?" People in Bethel are hurting. In 2011, they were paying $6.87 a gallon for gasoline, and stove oil prices were also expensive. In addition, with the economic downturn, cuts were being made in social services to rural villages. Ms. McEachern said, "And right now, they're proposing here the largest gold mine in human history, the Pebble Mine, that's going to do catastrophic damage to the environment and the native community, in the premier wild salmon habitat in the world. So I'm not well-versed on the larger economic system, but I can relate to the idea of corporate wealth being lopsidedly in the hands of so few, when so many are struggling." Ms. McEachern said she was surprised that the photo went viral: "I didn't think anything was going to explode like this. I didn't really quite get a clue until I opened my Facebook one morning, and there's over 200 friend requests. I've got to tell you, I'm likeable, but not that likeable." Of course, not everyone liked the photo, and some people posted negative comments. She said, "For those who ask about the [permanent fund dividend] that all Alaskans receive [based on oil revenues], I got mine and donated it to Greenpeace on behalf of Glenn Beck. To the suggestion I set myself on fire, [I wrote,] 'I AM on fire!'"[8]

• The 4th Amendment to the United States Constitution says this: "The right of the people to be secure in their persons, houses, papers, and effects, against unreasonable searches and seizures, shall not be violated, and no Warrants shall issue, but upon probable cause, supported by Oath or affirmation, and particularly describing the place to be searched, and the persons or things to be seized." Many people consider X-rays that show their private parts during Homeland Security screenings at airports to be a violation of their civil rights. One way to silently protest this loss of our precious freedom is to wear 4th Amendment underwear. This underwear has the 4th Amendment printed in metallic ink on undershirts and underwear. The metallic ink is supposed to make the 4th Amendment show up on airport scanners. What about children? Should strangers be allowed to look at children's private parts at airports? Children can wear 4th Amendment underwear that says this: "READ THE 4TH AMENDMENT, PERVERTS." The people who invented this idea say this: "We found metallic type that could, in theory, show up on TSA scanners that would display the 4th Amendment. The clothes are designed as a silent protest against the new reality of being searched to the point where we're basically naked. We don't intend for this to be anything more than a thought-provoking way to fuel the debate about safety vs. civil liberties. If we sell a few items, great. But the main intention is to open more dialogue. It's more of a conceptual piece than anything else."[9]

• In 2010, General Electric reported worldwide profits of $14.2 billion. Last year, you reported personal income of how much? Who paid more in USAmerican federal income tax? Chances are, you did. Why? Because in 2010 General Electric paid no USAmerican federal corporate income tax, according to a 24 March 2011 *New York Times* article by David Kocieniewski. (Neither did Bank of America, which got a $336 billion bailout in 2009 and paid no USAmerican federal corporate income tax in 2010. These facts upset lots of patriotic USAmericans who pay their fair share of taxes, and some began writing or rubber-stamping messages on $1 bills. One message says, "This is $1 more than GE has paid in taxes." Another says, "This is $1 more than the Bandits of America (BOA) paid in taxes." One way to show that you love your country is to pay your fair share of taxes.[10]

Advertising

• After winning $30,000 in the 1978 Burger King Open in Miami, Florida, professional bowler Randy Lightfoot was asked by a TV announcer if he would use any of his winnings to buy Whoppers at Burger King. He replied, "No," and Burger King very quickly dropped its sponsorship of professional bowling tournaments.[11]

• Heywood Broun once reviewed a Broadway comedy as "a triumph of dullness and vulgarity." Immediately, the advertisements for the comedy blared "'A triumph' — Broun in the 'Tribune.'"[12]

Advice

• A man once came to Rabbi Yehudah Asad to ask his advice. The man explained that he wished to buy a run-down store, fix it up, and make his living from it. The Rabbi advised him not to buy the store. Later, a different man came to the Rabbi to ask about the same store. He said that he wished to buy the run-down store, fix it up with the help of God, and make his living from it. The Rabbi advised him to buy the store. Later, the first man came to the Rabbi and asked about the difference in advice. The Rabbi explained that the second man would ask for the help of God in fixing up the store, whereas the first man had wanted to fix up the store without the help of God. A person who has help from God has an excellent chance of making a success.[13]

• Very often, an actor would have trouble with part of his role, whether it was speaking a line or performing some piece of business, and he would go to theatrical director Tyrone Guthrie for help. Often, Mr. Guthrie would have the answer at hand, but if he did not, he would tell the actor, "Go home, think about it, come back, and astonish us in the morning." Mr. Guthrie also uttered another characteristic quote whenever problems arose in the theater — he would tell the cast and crew, "Rise above."[14]

Alcohol

• Tenor Jussi Bjoerling and conductor Nils Grevilius enjoyed having a drink together — and another drink, and another, and on and on. During one debauch, they traveled together to Stockholm, where to take a break from their drinking, they decided to go to the opera house and see whatever was being performed. They got to their seats and waited and waited, and were about to leave and get some more drinks when the opera house general manager came on stage and announced that that evening's performance was being canceled because "tenor Jussi Bjoerling and conductor Nils Grevilius are missing." A very surprised Mr. Bjoerling and Mr. Grevilius stood up and announced, "We're here! We're here!"[15]

• George Washington once signed a mock contract with his gardener. The contract provided money for the gardener to get drunk and specified for how long the gardener could remain drunk.

According to the contract, the gardener was to receive "four Dollars at Christmas, with which he may be drunk 4 days and 4 nights; two Dollars at Easter to effect the same purpose; two Dollars also at Whitsontide, to be drunk two days; A Dram in the morning, and a drink of Grog at Dinner or at Noon."[16]

• Irish playwright Brendan Behan enjoyed drinking to excess. He once said, "As regards the drink, I can only say that when I was growing up drunkenness was not regarded as a social disgrace. To get enough to eat was regarded as an achievement. To get drunk was a victory." By the way, Mr. Behan once met an acquaintance in a pub and asked, "I hear there's someone dead belonging to you — it's not yourself by any chance?"[17]

• Richard Brinsley Sheridan had a financial interest in the Drury Lane Theatre, which caught on fire on February 24, 1809. Mr. Sheridan heard about the fire and then went to the theater and watched it burn as he drank in the Piazza Coffee-House. A friend was amazed at Mr. Sheridan's calmness as he watched his theater burn, but Mr. Sheridan said, "A man may surely be allowed to take a glass of wine at his own fireside."[18]

Animals

• In October 2011 in Wasau, Wisconsin, fire broke out at the home of Kim Carlson and her fiancé, Todd Borchardt. Ms. Carlson said that when she discovered that Koda, the family's seven-year-old yellow Labrador retriever, was still in the burning house, "My first reaction was to go upstairs and check upstairs, but it was just entirely too smoky. It was so black that you couldn't see anything in front of you. My first reaction was that I wanted to cover myself in water and cover my face and mouth and go up and get him myself, knowing that's not the right thing to do." Firefighter Jamie Giese said that the firefighters "found Koda in the very last room they searched, which happened to be the room that was actually on fire." Koda was carried unconscious out of the house. Mr. Giese said, "I told [fellow firefighter]

Jared [Thompson] that we've got to work this dog. [We] laid him down in the front yard, and we started assisting breathing." Mr. Giese revived the pet dog with mouth-to-snout resuscitation. Mr. Giese said, "I have never been trained in that. I've seen it on TV and pictures in the newspapers and things like that. We thought [the dog] was dead. We could tell he was trying to breathe, and our training for humans is airway, breathing, circulation. We had no tools handy, so it was mouth-to-snout." After Koda started breathing again, he was given oxygen and other treatment. He recovered fully. Koda had been a member of the Giese family for only four days before the fire. The Gieses said that they saw his photograph in an advertisement and they fell in love with him.[19]

• In the early 20th-century play *Palmy Days* is a scene in which a dog recognizes a character named "Kaintuck" in a saloon. The scene worked very well on stage. The playwright trained his dog to find his hat. He told his dog, "Where's that hat?" and the dog would search for the hat, howling until he found it. On opening night, the playwright gave the hat to the actor playing Kaintuck, and for the recognition scene, he told his dog, "Where's that hat?" The audience heard howling offstage and then saw the dog come on stage and go directly to Kaintuck, who was wearing the hat.[20]

• Downhill mountain bike racer Missy Glover loves pets. While racing, she carries her dead dog's ashes, and around her neck she wears the taxidermist-preserved remains of another deceased pet — a piranha. She also believes in meditation, and for that purpose, she built a Mongolian yurt in her backyard.[21]

• Animals cause their share of mishaps on stage. Fred Terry once wore a false nose while playing the role of King Charles, who kept a number of spaniels. During a performance, one of the spaniels jumped up, bit off the end of the false nose and then ran away. The audience was delighted.[22]

• In a Central Village cemetery in Connecticut is a tombstone bearing the inscription, "ROSA. My first Jersey Cow. Record 2 lbs. 15 ozs. Butter. From 18 qts 1 day milk."[23]

Art and Artists

• The Taliban is against much art. In 1996, the Taliban rose to power in Afghanistan and immediately forbade paintings that depicted animals or humans. An Afghan physician named Muhammad Yousef Asefi, who was also an artist, wished to preserve this kind of art. Therefore, he used watercolor to paint over animals and humans, thereby disguising them. Dr. Asefi said about the Taliban, "They were determined to destroy the culture of Afghanistan. Gradually, step by step, they would have come around to destroying my paintings." After the Taliban fell from power in Afghanistan in 2001 (the Taliban returned to power in Afghanistan in 2021), Dr. Asefi used a wet sponge to remove the watercolor and restore the paintings to their original condition. Dr. Asefi said about the removal of the watercolor, "Taking it off is easy." However, he added, "Putting it on was very difficult." Dr. Asefi preserved much art for future generations to see.[24]

• Pablo Picasso created his mural *Guernica* to protest the 26 April 1937 bombing of the Basque village Guernica by Fascists using German airplanes. The planes killed 1,654 and wounded 889 of the village's population of 7,000. During World War II, when the Nazis occupied France, Picasso stayed in Paris. Frequently, the police came to his studio, but he simply smiled and gave them postcards picturing his *Guernica*. Once, a German officer asked him about *Guernica*, "Did you do this?" Picasso replied, "No, you did."[25]

• While living and painting at Zaandam, which is near Amsterdam, Impressionist painter Claude Monet bought some groceries and carried them home, where he discovered that they had been wrapped in paper that was actually a work of art — a brilliantly colored Japanese wood-block print. Mr. Monet went back to the grocery store and bought the rest of the prints, thus starting a collection that greatly influenced his own art.[26]

• Artist James Abbott McNeill Whistler was once asked why he was so rude to so many people. He replied, "Early in life I made the discovery that I was charming, and if one is delightful, one has to thrust the world away to keep from being bored to death."[27]

Audiences

• When he was a young man acting in England, Jerome K. Jerome traveled with a troupe that had only one backdrop for representing a cottage interior. In one particular play, it had to be used to represent the interiors of four different cottages — the actors simply altered the on-stage furniture while using the same backdrop. Unfortunately, some audience members weren't amused by the play, so they decided to amuse themselves with the backdrop. Whenever a couple of scenes had passed without the use of the backdrop, audience members called out to ask about its welfare and whether it had been lost, and whenever the backdrop made a belated appearance, the audience cheered and shouted, "Who said it was lost?"[28]

• John Gielgud and Mrs. Patrick Campbell once played to nearly empty houses in Ibsen's *Ghosts*, and so Mrs. Campbell occasionally remarked to Mr. Gielgud on stage, "The Marquis and Marchioness of Empty are in front again."[29]

Baseball

• In 1905, one of baseball's greatest fans attended a Detroit game. In the 11th inning of a closely contested game, the umpire, Jack Sheridan, was given a message to announce to the spectators: "Is S.D. Reed in the stands? He is wanted at home. His house is on fire." Mr. Reed was in the stands, but he replied, "I'm not leaving. I couldn't get home in time to do anything about the fire anyway, so let the damn house burn."[30]

• One of the best baseball batters of all time is Stan Musial. Joe Garagiola once caught for a young pitcher who was facing Mr. Musial.

Mr. Garagiola kept giving signs for pitches, but the pitcher kept shaking them off. Finally, Mr. Garagiola went to the pitcher's mound and asked the young pitcher what he wanted to throw against Mr. Musial. "Nothing," the pitcher replied. "I want to hold the ball as long as possible."[31]

• Baseball manager Dick Williams was not popular. He was thrown out of a game one night, and he was so mad at the beginning of the next game that he wouldn't come out of the dugout to give the umpires his starting lineup. Instead, he sent out a pitcher, Bryn Smith, to do it. Mr. Smith greeted the umpires by saying, "Any chance of throwing him out again?"[32]

Books

• James Abbott McNeill Whistler did not write the title of his book, *The Gentle Art of Making Enemies*. At first, Mr. Whistler had intended to have a man named Sheridan Ford research his letters to editors and get credit for publishing them, but then he decided to have them published himself. Mr. Ford then proceeded to try to publish a pirated text of Mr. Whistler's correspondence with the media. A printer in Antwerp, Belgium, disliked Mr. Ford's original title, *The Correspondence of James McNeill Whistler*, and choose to use as a title six words from Mr. Ford's introduction to the book. Mr. Whistler found out about the pirated edition of the book and suppressed it, but he helped himself to Mr. Ford's title.[33]

• Isaac Asimov wrote his autobiography for Doubleday, but after writing 50 pages, he discovered that he had gotten only as far as his first three years of life, meaning that his autobiography would be huge. His friend and fellow science-fiction writer Ben Bova visited him and saw the many pages of typed manuscript that Mr. Asimov was pouring out. Mr. Asimov explained, "In this autobiography, I'm including every stupid thing I can remember having said or done." Mr. Bova joked, "No wonder it's so long."[34]

Charity

• A man once came to the city of Kovno, pretended to be a beggar, and collected a large amount of money. However, the people of Kovno learned that the man was only pretending to be a beggar and in fact was quite wealthy. Therefore, the city council of Kovno determined to pass a law banning beggars from the city. When the Rabbi of Kovno, Yitzchak Elchanan Specter (1817-1896), heard about the proposed law, he said to the city council, "Who deceived you? A needy person or a wealthy person? It was a wealthy person feigning poverty. If you want to make an ordinance, it should be to ban wealthy persons, not needy beggars, from collecting alms."[35]

• A man came to Yogi Berra's home to repair the venetian blinds, but Yogi didn't know he was coming. When his son told him, "Dad, the guy is here for the venetian blinds," he replied, "Look in my pants pocket and give him five bucks."[36]

Children

• Beverly Cleary, the author of the Henry, Ribsy, Beezus, and Ramona series of novels for children, was an artist at a very young age. Someone left a pot of ink — people used pots of ink to write back then — on top of a table with a white tablecloth. Young Beverly poured some of the ink on the table, dipped her hands in the ink, and went around the tablecloth making prints of her hands. In addition to being an artistic child, she was a curious child. When her father butchered a hog, young Beverly was forbidden to go outside and watch so she went to an upstairs window and watched the butchering from a distance. By the way, she knew that she enjoyed writing. When she was married, she and her husband moved to the hills by Berkeley, California. Moving into the house, they found reams of typing paper that the previous owners had left behind. Beverly told her husband that she would like to write a book but that she needed a sharp pencil. The next day her husband gave her a gift: a pencil sharpener. Her first book was published in 1950: *Henry Huggins.*[37]

• Film critic Roger Ebert attended a Catholic school. Each year, the school held a magazine subscription contest, with part of the proceeds going to the school. (Roger won the contest two years in a row.) The Curtis Circulation Company sponsored the contest, and a Curtis pitchman told the students, "Everyone you know is a sales opportunity! Your parents, your neighbors, even people you meet! Don't be shy! Sell those subscriptions!" Young Roger raised his hand and asked, "Sir, would you like to buy a subscription?" (Here's another Roger story: At St. Joseph's Camp for Boys, he had a friend who wore glasses. Other friends took this friend's glasses, put them on, and staggered around and pretended that they were blind. When Roger put on the glasses, suddenly the world appeared in focus, and he did not want to take off the glasses. He wrote his parents, "I need glasses!")[38]

• As a 13-year-old boy, Colin Powell attended a Catholic summer camp near Peekskill, New York. He and some other boys smuggled beer into the camp and hid it, but the beer was quickly discovered. At the camp meeting hall, the priest in charge talked to the campers, told them about the beer, and asked, "Who will own up like a man?" Colin was sure that no one had seen him and the other boys smuggle the beer into the camp, but he thought about the priest's words and confessed. As a result of Colin's example, two other guilty boys confessed as well. For their punishment, Colin and the other boys were sent home, but a priest called Colin's parents and told them that Colin had owned up like a man and had been a good example to the other guilty boys.[39]

• As you may expect, science-fiction writer Isaac Asimov was a precocious child. He even taught himself to read. His father was proud of him and said to Isaac's Uncle Joe, "Isaac can find any word in the dictionary." Uncle Joe replied, "Impossible!" Isaac looked up the word "impossible" in the dictionary and showed it to Uncle Joe. Later, Isaac ran into a problem. He showed off his intelligence in school, and some bullies disliked him because of that and so they beat him up. Isaac solved this problem by doing the homework of the biggest bully, who then kept the other bullies from beating him up.[40]

• Hillary Rodham Clinton and her brother were not pampered when they were growing up — for one thing, they did not receive an allowance. Hillary's brother, Tony, remembers doing chores around the house and then at dinner asking their father for a few dollars. However, having grown up during the Depression, their father was not free with money. Instead, he would give Tony an extra potato and say, "That's your reward." Hillary's father was hard to please. Hillary would come home from school with a report card full of A's, and her mother would be pleased and say, "Oh, that's wonderful, dear." However, her father would say, "You must go to a pretty easy school."[41]

• As a small child, Christina Lessa became entranced by gymnastics and started taking lessons. After a whole week of lessons, she decided to perform an Olympic-level balance beam dismount that takes years to learn. She broke her wrist and gave up her lessons, but as an adult she became a renowned photographer of gymnasts.[42]

• When Muhammad Ali, nee Cassius Clay, was an infant, some of the first sounds he made were "gee-gee." After he grew up and became a world-famous boxer, he claimed that he had been trying to say "Golden Gloves." (Mr. Ali won the national amateur boxing tournament known as Golden Gloves twice in his career.)[43]

• Obviously, the White House is very concerned about security. When Caroline Kennedy's pet hamsters escaped from their cage, JFK's press secretary, Pierre Salinger, announced at a press conference, "Our security is very tight, but these were extremely intelligent hamsters."[44]

• A Presbyterian family once visited a Baptist church where the family's young daughter was very impressed by a stained glass window portraying Jesus. The daughter said, "I always knew God was a Presbyterian — but I didn't know until today that Jesus was a Baptist."[45]

• Performance artist Rinde Eckert identifies his pivotal performance as the time he played Peter Rabbit while he was in kindergarten. Whenever he dipped his head so that his bunny ears flopped over his face, the audience laughed.[46]

Church

• Abraham Lincoln once ran for Congress against pioneer preacher Peter Cartwright. Once, Mr. Lincoln attended one of his rival's sermons. Mr. Cartwright asked everybody who wished to go to Heaven to stand up. Almost everyone stood up. Then he asked everybody who wished to avoid going to H*ll to stand up. At this point, everybody but Mr. Lincoln was standing. Mr. Cartwright then said, "I observe that many of you accepted my invitation to give their hearts to God and go to Heaven. I further observed that all but one of you indicated an aversion to going to H*ll. The sole exception is Mr. Lincoln, who failed to respond to either invitation. May I inquire of you, Mr. Lincoln, where you are going?" Mr. Lincoln replied, "I'm going to Congress."[47]

• Comedian Dick Van Dyke, who used to be a Sunday School teacher, once imagined a want ad for a Sunday School teacher: "Wanted: Teacher. Must have the wisdom of Solomon, the patience of Job, the courage of David. Must teach like St. Paul, lead like Moses, and stay cool under fire like Shadrach." By the way, Mr. Van Dyke and his wife taught their young children to say this prayer: "Lord, we thank Thee for our food, for rest and home and all things good, for wind and rain and Heaven above, but most of all for those we love."[48]

• Calvin Coolidge attended church alone one Sunday. When he returned home, his wife asked him what the preacher had spoken about in his sermon. "Sin," Coolidge replied. Next his wife asked, "What did he have to say about it?" Coolidge answered, "He was against it."[49]

Class

• During World War II, USAmerican heavyweight champion Joe Louis predicted that the Allies would win. Why? Because, he said, we are on the side of God. This is an improvement on the opinion of people who believed that we would win because God is on our side. Mr. Louis showed a lot of class throughout his career. A reporter once heard a couple of residents of Harlem talking. One said, "If we had more Negroes like Joe Louis, things would be better for us." The other replied, "True, but if we had more white folks like Joe, things would be better still."[50]

• Believe it or not, at the 1991 World Figure Skating Championships, figure skater Midori Ito jumped right out of the skating rink. She fumbled for a moment with a TV camera and then went back out onto the ice and skated as if nothing unusual had occurred.[51]

Chapter 2: From Clothing to Guns

Clothing

• Golfer Walter Hagen had a reputation for partying. According to legend, he sometimes showed up at tee time in a wrinkled tuxedo because he had been partying all night and didn't have time to change. The truth is quite different. Mr. Hagen was often seen at parties with a glass in his hand, but when he had to play in a tournament the next day, he tossed the drink into a potted plant and then went home to get a good night's sleep. His tuxedo got wrinkled because he ordered his chauffeur to roll it into a ball and throw it against the car until it was wrinkled enough to carry on the legend.[52]

• Back in the 1970s, when Mary Bacon was riding professionally in horse races, the flower print of her underwear could be seen through her jockey outfit's white bottoms. She used to tell the other jockeys, "At least I give you something to look at when I'm in the lead."[53]

• Noël Coward showed up for a dinner party wearing white tie and tails, only to discover that the other guests were wearing casual clothing. He apologized, "So sorry for being improperly dressed."[54]

• Tennis star Arthur Ashe could afford to wear very expensive clothing, but his favorite piece of clothing was a simple T-shirt bearing this slogan: "A citizen of the world."[55]

Critics

• Oscar Wilde once went into a florist shop and asked that the flowers in the window be removed. The florist replied, "With pleasure, sir. How many would you like to have?" Mr. Wilde replied, "Oh, I don't want any, thank you. I only asked to have them removed from the window because I thought that they looked tired." By the way, Mr. Wilde once said about an actress who had married a fool: "She thought that, because he was stupid, he would be kindly, when, of course, kindliness requires imagination and intellect."[56]

• When George S. and Beatrice Kaufman celebrated their fifth anniversary — the wooden one — critic Alexander Woollcott sent them this telegram: "I have been looking around for an appropriate wooden gift and am pleased hereby to present you with Elsi Ferguson's performance in her new play."[57]

• David Garrick, the famous 18th-century actor, believed in using his entire body while playing a part. He once criticized the French actor P.L.D. Preville after appearing on stage with him in a drunk scene — he said that although most of Mr. Preville's body was drunk, his legs were not![58]

Death

• In 1986, nurse anesthetist Kathleen Hanna assisted in an operation on a 47-year-old man who had suffered from an acute myocardial infarction. He was nervous about the necessary upcoming operation and talked to nurse Hanna about his 13-year-old daughter and how much he loved her and the other members of his family. The operation went badly, and the physician realized that the patient needed to be made unconscious for the rest of the operation. The patient then told nurse Hanna, "Please tell my family I love them." The patient died on the operation table, but nurse Hanna wrote later, "I went to his family after the surgeon had spoken with them and gave them [the patient's] message. These were the last words he said — his final thought. The family said it gave them some comfort, and I was glad to be able to deliver it to them."[59]

• Wisdom can be ancient, or modern. This ancient wisdom comes from the *Ecclesiastes Rabbah* 5:14: A fox wanted to eat some grapes in a vineyard, but he was unable to squeeze through a narrow opening in the fence. Therefore, he fasted for three days, and once he had slimmed down, he ate his fill of grapes. However, the fox discovered that he was unable to get out of the vineyard because he was too fat to squeeze through the narrow opening in the fence. Therefore, the fox again fasted for three days so he could get outside the vineyard. Once outside of the vineyard, the fox turned around and said, "Vineyard, vineyard, how good is your fruit! All that is within you is beautiful and worthy of praise. But of what use are you? Just as one enters you, one must come out." As one enters and leaves the vineyard, so one enters and leaves life.[60]

• In 1975, nurse Kelly Gaul had an elderly patient who was dying of lung cancer and who often had radiation treatment. However, one day he said that he did not want to have the radiation treatment: Being moved was painful, and the table he was put on for radiation treatment was hard. He wanted to get cleaned up, wear clean pajamas, and spend time with his wife. Nurse Kelly told him that he could skip the radiation treatment — although the radiologist was furious — and she got him cleaned up and put clean pajamas on him. He spent time with his wife and died that afternoon. She then sat quietly with his wife, who held her hand. Nurse Kelly writes, "Somewhere, somehow, I, like so many other nurses, decided that patients and moments were what mattered."[61]

• Henry Rollins says that he is not especially brave, but that he does not have much fear. While he was in Iraq, he was in a building signing autographs for the troops. Bombs started hitting the building, and a soldier told him, "Sir! You're in a fortified building! You're in *no* danger!" Mr. Rollins said, "Cool!" Then he signed more autographs. The soldier asked him, "Sir! You're not scared?" Mr. Rollins replied, "Oh, I'm scared. I just don't really care when I die." He made an impression on the soldier, who said to him, "Sir? Uh ... that's really f**ked up."[62]

• In the Old cemetery in Washington, New Hampshire, is a grave monument that says, "Capt. Samuel Jones' Leg which was amputated July 7 1804." The rest of Captain Jones is buried on Rhode Island, where he moved after having his leg amputated.[63]

• As a newspaper reporter in the early 20th century, Ben Hecht witnessed many executions — all hangings. He remembers at one hanging, a condemned man was asked if he had any last words. The condemned man replied, "Not at this time."[64]

Do It Yourself

• Many bands, including punk bands, are Do It Yourself. In her book *Girls to the Front: The True Story of the Riot GRRRL Revolution*, Sara Marcus explains, "DIY was a philosophy and a way of life, a touchstone that set its industrious adherents apart from the legions of USAmericans who passed their lives — as the punks saw it — trudging from TV set to first-run multiplex, from chain record store to commercial radio dial, treating art and culture as commodities to be consumed instead of vital forces to be struggled with and shaped, experimented with and created, breathed and lived." An example of a Do-It-Yourself band was Bratmobile. Quite simply, Allison Wolfe, Molly Neuman, and Erin Smith met and started making music. Previously, Erin was interesting in being only a fan: "I had to be the best fan possible; it never occurred to me to be anything else." But the three met and very quickly wrote a song together. Sara Marcus writes, "The thrill! It could happen! It didn't even have to be hard! The universe was full of songs, just waiting for you to get some friends together and write them. And then you weren't just a fan anymore; you were a member of the fellowship of people who made things." Very quickly, they decided to play their song ("Stab") in public at Maxwell's in Hoboken, New Jersey, where they had gone to see some bands, including Nation of Ulysses. The other bands were very supportive of Bratmobile. Erin remembers, "They were just like, '*Of course* you're going to play our guitars.'" Bratmobile played their song, but in the middle of performing it they realized that they had forgotten to write an ending for it. Of course, the ending on stage resembled a crash landing, but it didn't matter. Even if some of the non-creating members of the audience were wondering what Bratmobile was doing on stage, Bratmobile heard plenty of cheers from the people who were creators.

Bratmobile practiced three more times, and they wrote five more songs, and then they recorded the songs. In DIY, things can happen fast.[65]

Education

• Soviet leader Leonid Brezhnev was known for his ignorance in general and his ignorance of the arts in particular — a fact that underground humorists used in jokes such as this: When he died, he went to the gates of Heaven, but St. Peter asked him for proof of identity. When Brezhnev asked how he could prove who he was, St. Peter gave a few examples: "If Pablo Picasso came, he could paint a picture. If Arthur Rubinstein came, he could play the piano. If Maria Callas came, she could sing." Puzzled, Brezhnev asked, "Who are Picasso, Rubinstein, and Callas?" St. Peter laughed and then said, "Now I am sure who you are — you have got to be Brezhnev."[66]

• What counts as a good education varies from culture to culture. Some white USAmerican settlers once took some youths of the Six Nations, gave them an education, and then returned them to the Native Americans. However, the Native Americans were dissatisfied because the youths knew nothing about hunting and trapping, or about making war. Therefore, the Native Americans approached the white settlers to say that if the whites should give them some youths to be educated, they would make sure the youths learned the important things in life.[67]

• Zusia and Elimelekh were brothers and Hasidic masters. After they had become famous, they traveled to a certain town, where a rich man offered them lodging at his mansion. Zusia said to the rich man, "Previously, whenever we traveled to this town, we stayed with a poor farmer who offered us hospitality when you did not. Why do you now offer us hospitality? Is it because of our horses and carriages? Then invite our horses to stay at your mansion — we shall stay with the poor farmer."[68]

• Lots of teachers find their jobs rewarding. Syndicated columnist Connie Schultz met a teacher who told her about a young boy who lagged far behind his peers in reading. The teacher worked with the boy for months, and finally the boy read out loud an entire page by himself. The teacher said, "I wish you could have seen his face. He put his book on his lap, raised both hands in the air, and shouted, 'I can read! I can read!'"[69]

• As a young girl, future Secretary of State Madeleine Albright attended the Kent School for Girls in Denver, Colorado, where she once won an 8th-grade contest by listing all 51 member states of the United Nations in alphabetical order. At every school she attended, she started a new club to study foreign policy — she admits that one advantage of starting a new club is that you can name yourself president.[70]

• Four novices made a vow of silence, and then they sat meditating around a candle. A gust of air blew out the candle, so the first novice said, "The candle has gone out." The second novice said, "Be quiet. We're not supposed to talk." The third novice said, "Why are you talking?" And the fourth novice said, "I'm the only one who didn't say anything."[71]

• After becoming First Lady in 1992, Hillary Rodham Clinton spoke before a group of talented high school students, then asked for questions. The boys waved their hands in the air, but the girls sat quietly with their hands by their sides. Ms. Clinton waited for a while, and then said, "I'm looking for a woman's hand."[72]

• Gymnasts tend to be small. When Kurt Thomas was a hall monitor in school, he worked with another boy named Elvis Peacock, who became a star football player at Oklahoma. Mr. Thomas remembers, "If I asked a guy for his pass when Peacock wasn't around, it was like I wasn't even there."[73]

• Frank Carroll coached figure skater Linda Fratianne, whom he called "the perfect student, because she would listen and try to do exactly what she was told. If I asked her to jump off a roof, she would say, 'This roof? Or that higher roof?'"[74]

• In 1981, elite gymnastics coaches Bela and Marta Karolyi defected from Romania to the United States. Neither knew English, but they learned the language by watching *Sesame Street*.[75]

Etiquette

• The Barrymores — Lionel, Ethel, and John — were very formal when they were around each other. This shocked one of their acquaintances, who asked, "My God, don't you know each other?" By the way, the Barrymores' father, Maurice, enjoyed drinking to excess, and he once stated, "Staggering is a sign of strength. Weak men are carried home."[76]

• There is a certain etiquette — and attention to safety — in pairs figure skating. For example, if the man is holding the woman high in the air and something happens so that she falls, proper etiquette requires that the man break her fall by allowing her to fall on top of him rather than directly onto the ice.[77]

• Dame Edith Evans was once asked to play Lady Macbeth, but she declined, saying, "It's absolutely out of the question. I could *never* impersonate a woman who had such a *peculiar* notion of hospitality."[78]

Fathers

• In 2010, graphic designer Anthony Herrera took his family on a trip to Sequoia National Park. He and his little daughter are fans of the *Star Wars* series of movies, and Mr. Herrera told his little daughter that Sequoia National Park was where the Ewoks — the teddy bear-like species that appeared in *Return of the Jedi* — lived. His little daughter kept looking for Ewoks, but unfortunately, she did not see any. Mr. Herrera explained to her that the Ewoks are a shy species and therefore few people ever see them. He took lots of photos during the trip, and when they got home, he used Photoshop to add hidden Ewoks to some of the photos. In Mr. Herrera's words, "After we got home, and after I had a little time alone with the photos, I told her I thought I saw something strange in a few pictures. We viewed them on the TV to get a larger image. You can imagine how surprised and excited she was when we discovered that we didn't see any Ewoks, but they saw us, and had certainly taken an interest in her and her little brother. Maybe I'm a little wrong for lying to her and falsifying the pictures, but I don't care. She'll never forget the time she spent in the big woods with Ewoks."[79]

• Pablo Picasso first learned about art from his father, Don José Ruiz Blasco, who would take a real pigeon's feet, pin them on a board, and have young Pablo draw them. Pablo also played a game with his young relatives. They would name an animal, and he would either draw it or cut it out of paper with scissors. Frequently, his father would start a drawing, then have his son finish it. When Pablo was 13 years old, he completed a drawing of a pigeon that his father had begun. His father looked at the drawing and realized that Pablo had surpassed him as an artist. Therefore, he gave his art supplies to his son and stopped creating art.[80]

• Even at six months old, Tiger Woods was learning how to be a golfer. As Tiger sat in a highchair, his father, Earl, demonstrated to him how to hit golf balls. When Tiger was old enough to swing his first golf club — a putter with the top of the handle sawn off — he wiggled the club twice before hitting the ball, exactly as his father was accustomed to do. His father says, "His first swing was a perfect imitation of mine. It was like looking at myself in a miniature mirror."[81]

• When young-people's author Jean Little was growing up, she liked to read and write, but her stories tended to be about elves, leading her father to advise her, "Write about what you know." She immediately wrote a story about a father and a daughter — and elves. But she discovered that she enjoyed writing about the father and daughter more than she did writing about the elves.[82]

Feminism

• At the very first modern Olympic Games in 1896, a woman named Melpomene wanted to compete in the marathon, but no women were allowed to compete back then. She ran anyway — not on the road the men ran on, but off to the side, so often she had no decent surface to run on. She finished one-and-a-half hours behind the winner.[83]

• Celebrated female jockey Julianne Krone was sometimes asked, "How does it feel to be a girl jockey?" She always replied, "Let's see, when I was a boy jockey it felt like that, and now that I'm a girl jockey it feels like this."[84]

Games

• Frank Benson was the manager of a traveling Shakespearean troupe and a lover of sports. He once sent a wire to an actor, asking, "Can you play Rugby tomorrow?" The actor wired back, "Yes," and arrived the next day expecting in play in a Rugby match — and was startled to learn that Mr. Benson wanted him to play the character of Rugby in *The Merry Wives of Windsor*.[85]

• As a young man, Rabbi Yechiel Michel of Gustinin decided to learn to play chess. However, he immediately quit after learning that one of the rules of chess was that a move, once made, cannot be taken back. Rabbi Michel explained that such a rule went against Judaism, which believes that no act is final. After one commits a sin, one can repent.[86]

Golf

• Even early in his career, golfer Sam Snead was able to drive the ball very well and very far. He once played Duke Gibson. On the first hole, Sam's ball went 25 yards further than Duke's ball, and Sam explained, "It must have hit a rock and bounced." The same result occurred on the second hole, and the third, and the fourth, and on each hole Sam made the same "explanation." An exasperated Duke finally asked Sam, "What the h*ll are you doing? Aiming at those d*mn rocks?"[87]

• In 1997, Tiger Woods won the Master's golf tournament and broke Jack Nicklaus' old record, becoming the first African-American and Asian-American to win the Master's. In 1975, the first

African-American golfer ever to play in the Master's was Lee Elder, who was present in 1997 when Tiger won. Tiger saw Mr. Elder and walked up to him to say, "Thanks for making this possible."[88]

• The caddies at the Royal and Ancient Golf Club at St. Andrews in Scotland weren't always literate. One caddy was seen "reading" a book at the caddie shelter, but another caddie pointed out that the book was upside down. The caddie with the book replied, "Any fool can read a book the right way up. It takes a good man to read it upside down."[89]

• Golfer Ben Hogan was famous for his powers of concentration on his own game. At the 1948 Masters, he played Claude Harmon. Playing the 12th hole, Mr. Hogan made a two, but Mr. Harmon made a hole in one. Afterward, Mr. Hogan said to Mr. Harmon, "That's the first time I've ever made a two there. What did you have, Charlie?"[90]

• A friend once took TV broadcaster Jim Burke to Kansas City's Hillcrest Country Club to play a round of golf, but Mr. Burke got off to a poor start. On the very first tee, he swung at the ball — and he missed. Then he adjusted his stand, took a swing at the ball — and he missed again. At this point, he told his friend, "Tough course!"[91]

• After Julie Foudy won an Olympic gold medal as a member of the United States women's national soccer team, she became a celebrity. One young girl wrote her, "I hope this is Julie Foudy the soccer player. You are my hero. Finally, I have a role model. If it wasn't for you, I'd probably have to play golf. I hate golf."[92]

Good Deeds

• A woman who calls herself "Moral12" when posting online at Helpothers.org wrote about a young woman — a foreign student — who had rented an unfurnished apartment and had nothing to put in it because of a lack of money. She even slept on the floor with only her coat to cover her. Moral12 telephoned the student and asked if she could bring over some free furniture and household items. The foreign student thanked her, and Moral12 began telephoning her friends. She writes, "One cleaned out her kitchen cabinets and provided pots and pans, some glassware, a jacket, a blanket. My mother raided her cabinets for items. My husband graciously consented to help play 'moving man' to transport our TV room loveseat, furniture cover, my daughter's twin bed, mattress, box springs, and more. My colleague here at work went out and purchased a brand-new comforter set, a small set of silverware, dishes and glasses." She and her husband then made three trips in their minivan and took the items to the foreign student. Moral12 writes, "She thanked me over and over again and could not believe that all these people whom she had not even met had given her all these things. I explained that people liked to help and that others had helped us in the past. She asked if there was anything she could do to repay us. I told her, 'Yes, there is one thing you can do for us: When you are in a position to help others, please remember to try and help.' With a smile on her face, she assured me that she would."[93]

• In October 2011, six-year-old Justice Wadsworth lost a teddy bear when she got sick while her family was driving along Interstate 90 on their way to Sedro-Woolley, Washington, after staying with a friend. Somehow, the teddy bear got left behind along the side of the Interstate. This was not just any teddy bear. Justice got it when she was little, and it was a gift from her father, a military man who serves overseas. Justice calls the teddy bear "Daddy Bear," and she said that "it makes her feel like she's cuddling with her daddy." Justice's mother, Christa, said that when the teddy bear turned up missing, "We searched the bedrooms. We called the friend we [had been] staying with. We cried and cried." Justice's grandmother posted a notice on Facebook about the lost teddy bear. The Washington Department of Transportation then tweeted about the teddy bear, including the location where it had been lost. Two Department of Transportation employees, Harry Nelson and Terry Kukes, went looking for the teddy bear and found it along the Interstate. They even drove, on their own time, to present the teddy bear to Justice in person. Justice said, "I was hoping" that someone would find the teddy bear. Christa said, "I'm so grateful," to Mr. Nelson and Mr. Kukes.[94]

• When John Adam was an eight-year-old boy, he and his younger sisters wanted to buy their mother a flower for Mother's Day. To raise money, they collected 18 soda pop bottles and got two cents for each bottle (a refund of the deposit). In addition, young John had three cents saved, and so they had a total of 39 cents. All together they walked to a florist shop, and young John put the money on the counter and asked if that would be enough to buy a flower for their mother for Mother's Day. The owner of the shop, young John remembers, "came over, looked us over, and said, 'Just a minute.' He went in back and came out with a geranium plant with gold foil wrapping around the pot. He took my three dimes, a nickel, and four pennies, and said, 'Thank you very much.' I had no idea that the cost was about four times as much. And we went proudly home carrying a flower plant for Mom."[95]

• A woman who uses the name "Jaybird" when posting on <HelpOthers.com> tells of a woman who worked at a local convenience store where Jaybird and her husband bought gas. One day the woman was not wearing her glasses because she had broken them and could not afford to buy a new pair. Unfortunately, the woman really, really needed eyeglasses. Jaybird and her husband thought about how they could help the woman, so they turned to their own optometrist, asking him to call the woman and have her come in for an eye exam and glasses and they would pay for everything. The optometrist did that, telling the woman that anonymous donors were paying for everything. The optometrist also waived the fee for the eye exam and reduced the price of the eyeglasses by 50 percent. The woman enjoyed telling her customers in the convenience store the story of how she got her new glasses.[96]

Guns

• Dave Marr and Tommy Bolt used to play against each other after making a friendly wager. Dave often lost, but despite not having much money, he was always able to pay off his losses by using merchandise he had won in amateur matches. After yet another loss to Tommy, Dave remembered that he had a shotgun in his trunk that he won at an amateur contest recently, and he thought that Tommy might be interested in it. So he got the shotgun and walked back to the clubhouse. Dave relates, "Tommy took one look at me coming through the door with a shotgun and almost died on the spot."[97]

• In his autobiography, *Standing the Gaff*, minor league umpire Harry "Steamboat" Johnson tells a story about umpiring a game in the Western League. It was the 9th inning, the bases were loaded, and a batter for the home team hit a high fly ball to left field. However, the cowboys in the crowd drew their guns and blasted the baseball to bits in the air before the visiting team's left fielder could catch the ball and make the out. What call should an umpire make in that situation? According to Steamboat, "You don't make calls like that against the home team!"[98]

Chapter 3: From Heroes to Names

Heroes

- In June 2007 in Allanville, Camperdown, North Tyneside, England, 10-year-old David John "DJ" Amers knew what to do when his mother, Beverley, stopped breathing and fell unconscious. He called 999 (Great Britain's emergency number), resuscitated her, and put her in the recovery position, all of which he had recently learned at his school. Beverley said, "I am so proud of DJ. He is my hero. He saved my life." Beverley had recently banged her head on something and passed out; she suffered a concussion. DJ said, "I was talking to the next-door neighbor, and my mother had gone to the shop to get a birthday card for a friend. She came back from the shop and couldn't speak. She was grabbing the fence and then she fell backwards. I quickly grabbed her things and rang 999 before giving her mouth to mouth and putting her in the recovery position." DJ's grandmother, Margaret Horrocks, said, "DJ came running around saying his mum had stopped breathing. I went after him but couldn't keep up. It was very scary, but DJ did such a good job and so did the school. The week before this happened, DJ put his teacher in the same position. Bless DJ, he did so well and was so controlled. But it was uncanny, I can't believe the school taught him in that short time some real-life skills. It is great that other children like DJ have these skills, so they can help in an emergency." DJ attends Burradon Primary School. Its Headmaster, Alistair Gilfillan, said, "We are very proud of DJ. We have recently provided First Aid training by the Red Cross for our children. DJ has obviously learnt from what he saw. These are vital life skills that we think are important children acquire from an early age." An ambulance service spokeswoman said, "It is very important that children of DJ's age know how to dial 999 and deal with a situation like this. DJ was extremely calm and brave under the circumstances and dealt with the situation remarkably."[99]

• In February 2011 in Milwaukie, Oregon, 24-year-old Jeff Bryant caught an infant and saved its life. Mr. Bryant heard an alarm as he walking to his car with a cup of coffee in his hand, and he walked toward the alarm to see what was going on. He saw a second-story apartment on fire — from a window leaned a woman, holding an infant. Mr. Bryant dropped his coffee and ran until he was directly under the infant. He yelled to the woman, "Drop the baby!" She yelled back, "Will you catch him?" He yelled, "Yes!" She dropped the baby, and Mr. Bryant, as he had promised, caught it. He said, "It was like catching an egg." He added, "He looked like he was sleeping. Just a baby in diapers." Steve McAdoo, spokesman for the Clackamas Fire Department, said, "It was an extremely hot and fast-moving fire. It was so intense that it blocked the exits for those inside." He praised Mr. Bryant: "It was fantastic. The woman was holding her baby out from the smoke and fire, and probably trying to figure out what to do. He stepped right up. I've never been around a case like this." The woman jumped from the window a few seconds after Mr. Bryant made his dramatic catch. The woman told firefighters that two other children were inside the building, but unfortunately firefighters were unable to revive those children. Mr. Bryant's wife called him a hero, but he is modest. He said, "To be honest. I just reacted. I didn't have time to be nervous." As a father of two young sons, he has had practice catching children. He said, "I play with them all the time by tossing them in the air. I know how to catch a child. I got the baby right under the armpits and then bent my knees to cushion the fall." He added, "I'm a father. I did what any father would do."[100]

• In November 2002, Dustin Baker, age 12, was at the Redlands Municipal Airport in Redlands, California. A pilot in a blue ultra-light aircraft took off, but it lost a wheel in the process. Without that wheel, the pilot would have a hard time landing the plane, and if the pilot did not know that the wheel was missing and tried to land the plane at the usual speed, the landing could be fatal. Dustin and a woman at the airport tried making a sign — "LANDING GEAR OFF" — to alert the pilot about the missing wheel, but the wind knocked it over. Therefore, Dustin grabbed the wheel and drove a yellow GMC truck equipped with sirens, lights, and fire extinguishers onto the runway. When the pilot approached the runway, Dustin turned on the truck's emergency lights and waved the wheel in the air to show the pilot that it had fallen off his plane. Dustin said, "When he flew by, I stood on top of the truck and showed the pilot the wheel." The pilot slowed down and landed safely. Pilot Randy Lehfeldt said about Dustin's action, "I think it was very heroic. He was a take-charge guy." He added, "Dustin's a hero in my eyes." Police spokeswoman Renee Groese said, "For a 12-year-old to be so alert and attentive to what's going on, he really did a great thing." Dustin's mother, Lita, said, "That's Dustin. He's so attentive and inquisitive. I'm not surprised, but I'm very proud." Lita added about her son, "He thought he was going to be arrested for driving the truck." However, police spokeswoman Renee Groese said, "The Police Department wants to recognize the achievements of people, especially young people, when they do good deeds such as these." Dustin's father, Steve, said, "We've always been extremely proud of him. He's a 45-year-old trapped in a 12-year-old's body."[101]

• In November 2005, Rosalia DeSantis, age 58, grew dizzy and fell onto a Toronto (Canada) Transit Commission subway track. Fortunately, Theo Parusis, age 25, and Alvaro Mejia, age 26, jumped onto the tracks and rescued her seconds before a train came into the station. The three people met later at Sunnybrook Hospital in Toronto. Ms. DeSantis stated, "I said, 'Thank you, because you are my angels. I'm so happy you were there at the time.' I think they're fantastic. I call them my angels. Yes, they are, they deserve all the credit." Mr. Mejia said, "I don't know what to say. I don't feel like a hero. I just saved a life." Mr. Parusis said, "I wouldn't say 'hero.' It's just a part of what we should be. If we all helped each other, it would be a much better place." Ms. DeSantis, a secretary, added, "I'm very happy they were there, and

I thank God they were there to help me." Mr. Parusis, a warehouse worker, remembered, "My initial reaction was to jump down and check if she was still alive. I tried to bring her up, but I struggled, so [Mr. Mejia] jumped down and attempted to help me. And an incoming train was coming. As soon as we saw the incoming train, we panicked, and we just got an adrenalin rush and managed to get her up in time. Five seconds later, the train just passed by." Mr. Mejia, who had arrived from Colombia two months previously as a refugee, said, "I didn't think [about] anything, I just tried to help him." Mr. Parusis said, "I just jumped, there's no thought. It all happened so quickly. Of course, if I was in that situation, I hope someone would do the same thing." Toronto Police Constable Scott Villers of 13 Division said that "what they did was incredible."[102]

• On 3 August 2003 in Oakland, California, Edie Dodds was driving a minivan that crashed after she felt her shoulder, she said, "pop out of its socket." The car hit another car and then rolled over, coming to a stop upside-down. Edie said, "The only thing that stopped us from going over the embankment was a parked Volvo." In the car with her were her nine-year-old son, Keither, and her six-year-old daughter, Eden. Keither smelled smoke and was worried about the minivan catching on fire. Edie was only semi-conscious after the accident, so Keither unbuckled her seat belt and his sister's seat belt to get them out of the minivan. He said, "I was sort of shocked. I've never been in an accident that bad. But all I thought about was helping my mom and my sister and trying to get out of the car." After getting his sister and his mother out of the minivan, Keither borrowed a cell phone and called his father, Oakland police officer Keith Dodds. Edie said, "The amazing part to me was that this little boy kept his composure throughout the whole thing." When Keither's father arrived, he was surprised to see that the minivan was totaled; Keither had been so calm on the phone that his father did not think that the accident had been as serious as it was. Keither, a 4th-grader, is a conflict manager at Joaquin

Miller Elementary. He said, "I solve problems as a conflict manager. I break up fights and help, like when my friend scraped his knee." He also once helped a little girl who was suffering an asthma attack. His father said, "I'm very proud of him. He worked through a serious emergency like that. I know conflict management has helped him."[103]

• In 2002 in St. Louis, Missouri, Doris Householder fell asleep while driving after working the night shift and crashed her pickup into the concrete base of a traffic sign. She was badly injured, and her pickup caught on fire. Ms. Householder remembers, "When I woke up, I could see four guys yelling to each other, 'Get away from the truck! It's going to blow up!' I'm screaming, 'No! Help! Don't let me burn alive!'" Coming to the rescue were Mary Whitehead, a homeless woman, and Bob Hughes, a local TV news photographer who arrived after hearing about the accident on a police scanner. Ms. Householder says, "Then I heard, 'It's okay, we're here!' And I see this black woman out the window." Ms. Whitehead and Mr. Hughes pulled Ms. Householder from the burning pickup. Mr. Hughes said, "I saw her foot hanging from the bone." He used a fast-food bag as a tourniquet, and surgeons later successfully reattached her foot. Ms. Householder said, "Bob kept me from bleeding to death. Mary kept me from freaking out to death" until the EMS arrived. Mr. Hughes said about his lifesaving action, "I just hope someone would do that for me or my wife." Ms. Whitehead had recently bought her daughter a Slushee at a nearby Phillips 66 for her 11th birthday, pointing out, "I had nothing else to give her," but the community rallied around her after her heroism became known. People donated $17,000 to her, and a nonprofit group found a five-bedroom ranch house for her and her family to live in.[104]

• In June 2007 Dale Newlands took a bicycle ride with his three children beside the River Lednock in Comrie, Perthshire, Scotland. He stopped to mend the bike of Georgia, his six-year-old daughter, while Connor, his 11-year-old son, and Gemma, his nine-year-old daughter, biked ahead. Unfortunately, Gemma's bike hit some large rocks and she and her bike went down the 20-foot bank and into the river. She was trapped underwater with the bike on top of her. Connor soon realized that Gemma was no longer behind him, and he investigated. When he saw Gemma and her bike in the river, he scrambled down the riverbank and went into the water. He was unable to lift the bike off Gemma, but he held her head out of the water so she could breathe until their father arrived and lifted the bike off her. The children's mother, Joanne, said, "I couldn't believe that a simple family cycle ride had turned into such a nightmare. Connor didn't want any fuss and was keen to play down his part in the whole drama. We're so proud of him. Connor saved his sister's life — it's as simple as that. Gemma thinks he is the best brother in the world. He's our hero, and we owe him everything."[105]

• Nine-year-old Scott Gonzales became a hero when he called 911 after his grandmother became seriously ill. He said, "She wasn't breathing. She was just really ill and it made me nervous, so I called the ambulance." Although other family members were present, Scott was the one who called 911. It turned out that his grandmother was suffering from a serious heart condition. Katherine Durham, a 911 operator, took Scott's call. She said, "He did good ... better than most of the adults. He was real calm, and I confirmed the address with them." Police chief Pete Alvarez presented Scott with the Corpus Christi (Texas) Police Department Citizens Lifesaving Certificate. Police Chief Alvarez said, "We do have heroes in the community — young and old. In this case, our hero is nine years old." Scott was staying with his grandmother because his parents were in Cancun. If Scott had gone with his parents to Cancun, he would not have been present to save his grandmother's life. Scott's father, Glen Gonzales, said, "He's glad we went away. If we hadn't gone, then his grandmother would have died, so I'm grateful he was there and knew what to do."[106]

• On 24 April 2002 in Phoenix, Arizona, a young woman snatched the purse of 58-year-old Mae Fields in a supermarket and then fled. Pursuing her was Melinda Haggan, a 48-year-old one-legged paraplegic in an electric wheelchair that one of her grandchildren modified so it could go 18 miles per hour. Ms. Haggan caught up with the purse-snatcher, sprayed her with pepper spray, and then dragged her by her hair back to the supermarket. In 1981, Ms. Haggan saw a teenager aim a pistol at a 12-year-old girl. She stepped in between the two and was shot — the bullet paralyzed her below the waist. Later, an ex-husband beat her so badly that one of her legs had to be amputated. Now she sells pencils. Ms. Fields always drops money into Ms. Haggan's cup. Ms. Fields said, "It was amazing that she would go to the lengths she did."[107]

Husbands and Wives

• On 29 September 2003, in Trinidad, Dale Ramnanan and his girlfriend, Lystra Ramkissoon, were accosted by bandits who tried to kidnap Lystra. Dale battled the bandits and rescued her. Two years later, they married. Dale said, "Our love grew. We became more attached. How could I marry someone else after that?" Lystra said, "I married my hero."

Dale worked as a chef at Imperial Garden Restaurant at Grand Bazaar, Trinidad, in the Caribbean, and at the time of the attack Lystra was a cashier there. Dale said, "We had just finished work around 10 p.m. and [were] waiting for transportation on the highway. It was hard getting a taxi. I wanted to drop Lystra home. A car pulled up. I sensed something was wrong even then, even as I was getting into the car. We sat in the back seat, I in the middle, a man on one side. We were driving along the highway and I [was] watching these three guys, [thinking] something wrong here.

"Suddenly, the guy in the front seat nod his head to the man in the back and push back his seat, pinning Lystra, and put a knife by her throat. The man next to me put a knife to my head and push my head between my legs." The car stopped at Carlsen Field, a farming community. Dale said, "The man next to me come out the car and drag me out. He say, 'Run, boy, or I will kill you.' But I was just coming at him. His knife was long, and he was running into me and I was stepping back. I didn't want them to go with Lystra."

The car started driving off, and the bandit jumped in the car. Dale said, "I tell myself I not giving her up. I ran to Lystra's side of the car. The [window] glass was halfway down. The car was speeding. I hold on to the door post and lock myself to the car. I was bumping off the road, so I climb a little higher, and put my hand in trying to open the lock, and the men only stabbing me on my arm to let go." Lystra said, "I was just whispering my prayers for the entire thing. When they stop the car and take out Dale, I see him coming back for me and dive on the car. I could see him trying to get the lock open. I heard this voice saying, 'Lystra, open the door and jump.'" She did exactly that.

After Lystra jumped out of the car, Dale also let go of the car door. Dale said, "As I hit the road, I got up. My little finger mash up but I ran to her. We started running, then she tell me her foot break, so we dive in the bush. The car stop and then the men ride out." Lystra's foot was badly broken — bone protruded from her flesh. Dale said, "I couldn't believe she run. She was bawling in pain, and I was trying to push the bone back in. When the car [was] gone, I put her on my back and continued the journey." They came to a house, and the residents allowed them to call for help. Dale and Lystra invited them to their wedding.

Lystra has a permanent limp, and Dale has knife scars on his arms, but he said, "I would do it all over again if I had to."

One person, other than Lystra, who is proud of Dale is his father, Narais Ramnanan, who said, "What my boy did was very brave to stand up to them and defend his girlfriend. It was love in his heart. They [the criminals] pushed him out of the car, but he did not run. Love brought him back to rescue her."[108]

• Before Janine Dunn married country and western singer Ronnie Dunn of Brooks and Dunn fame, he was married to someone else, and he told Janine, "I'm headed for divorce." Because she did not want to get involved with a married man, she replied, "When that happens, call me." Later, she was in the fiction section of a bookshop when a man who thought of himself as a psychic told her that she would love a tall and rangy man. Janine and her mother thought about who such a man could be, and the only tall and rangy man Janine knew was Ronnie Dunn. Janine told her mother, "It would be a cold day in h*ll before I'd marry him."[109]

• When she was in high school, Al Gore's wife, Tipper, used to play drums in an all-girl band called the Wildcats. It's no wonder that Secret Service agents gave her the code name "Skylark" when her husband was Vice President. By the way, sometimes, in-laws can be pushy. For a while, Al Gore's mother bought all of Tipper's clothing until Al made her stop. Also by the way, media representatives tend to always be present around such politicians and their wives as Al and Tipper Gore. In a comic protest, Tipper once soaked a few reporters with a water pistol.[110]

• Levi Yitzhak was a great believer and a great optimist who believed in being prepared. When his son was to be married, he sent out an announcement declaring that the wedding would be held at Jerusalem on a particular date at a particular time. The announcement then said, "But if, by chance, the Messiah will not yet have arrived, the wedding will take place on the same date and at the same time here in Berditchev."[111]

• Ellen Terry was a remarkably popular actress of the late 19th century. According to George Bernard Shaw, every theatergoer at one time or another fell in love with her. Agreeing, James Barrie, the author of *Peter Pan*, says that in the 1880s and 1890s, men sometimes proposed by saying, "As there's no chance of Ellen Terry marrying me, will you?"[112]

• Some country and western singers are very practical. For example, when one of Trace Adkin's early wives (not Rhonda) shot him, one of the things he immediately thought about was that he had new carpet and he did not want to bleed on it. So he walked over to a tile floor, collapsed, and bled on the tile.[113]

• In 1952, TV's Mister Rogers proposed to his wife, Joanne, in an unusual way: he wrote her a letter. She was so excited by the proposal that she called him on the telephone to accept. (At one time, long-distance telephone calls were a lot more expensive than they are now.)[114]

Illnesses and Injuries

• Disney will often invite young guests to be VIPs at such events as Disney ice shows. For example, in 2010, three-year-old Amber Saqib, a survivor of heart surgery, was a VIP guest at a Disney on Ice event in Newcastle, England. Performing on ice were characters from *Finding Nemo*, *The Incredibles*, *The Lion King*, *Pinocchio*, *Toy Story*, and more. As a VIP guest, Amber met Mickey and Minnie Mouse. Also attending the event were Amber's mother, Leanne, as well as Leanne's friend Joanne Stephenson, who is the mother of Amber's best friend, three-year-old Maisie. Leanne said, "We've been looking forward to it almost as much as the girls. We knew we were coming four weeks ago but didn't tell Amber until only about a week ago and she was so excited. She's been looking through the program at all the different things she wants to see." Amber's heart operation was successful and probably saved her life; fortunately, her heart condition was diagnosed early. Leanne said about Amber, "She's absolutely fine; she's just gone from strength to strength. You would never know apart from her scar. She calls it her 'magic zip.' I was dreading the surgery, but it's amazing to think how quickly she's made a recovery. I was a wreck for months before, but now she's come through the surgery it's as if I feel like a new person, too."[115]

• Major league umpire Bill Klem wore an inside chest protector, which afforded less protection than an outside chest protector, although Mr. Klem maintained that umpires could avoid injury by weaving with the ball. Even so, he once had his collarbone broken while umpiring. It healed, but it left a hole that you could stick your finger in. Later, fellow umpire Jocko Conlan had his collarbone broken while working a game. Mr. Klem told him, "You've got to weave." Mr. Conlan had roomed with Mr. Klem, and so he knew where the hole left by Mr. Klem's broken collarbone was located. He stuck his finger in the hole and said, "How did you get that?" Mr. Klem replied, "I didn't weave either, that day."[116]

• During Prohibition, medicinal alcohol was still legal. Workers in the Chrysler plant near Highland Park, Michigan, used to go to a certain doctor and tell him that they were suffering from "shaky nerves." The doctor knew exactly what would calm their nerves — he would immediately write out a prescription for a pint of whiskey. A drugstore located one floor below the doctor's office filled the prescription.[117]

• Strange, unusual, and true: A career in opera can end quickly. French mezzo Simone Berriaux once choked on a peppercorn while eating a beefsteak. Although she coughed repeatedly, she could not dislodge the peppercorn from beside her vocal cords. The next morning a surgeon removed the peppercorn, but it had damaged her vocal cords so badly that she was forced to retire from opera.[118]

• While umpiring a Pittsburgh Pirates game, Ken Burkhart saw a woman fan being carried out on a stretcher, so he asked the Pirates third-base coach, "What happened to her?" The third-base coach replied, "You called one right, and she fainted."[119]

Language

• After Thomas Jefferson wrote the Declaration of Independence, it was sent to the Continental Congress to be debated. Members of the Congress made many suggestions concerning changes they wanted made to the wording. Benjamin Franklin could see that Mr. Jefferson did not like many of the suggested changes, although he sat quietly, so Mr. Franklin told a story about a hatter named John Thompson, who decided to open a store and sell hats. Mr. Thompson wrote down his idea for a sign he wanted to have made, but he asked his friends to look over the wording first to ensure that it was suitable. The wording said: "John Thompson, Hatter, makes and sells hats for ready money." In addition, Mr. Thompson drew a picture of a hat. The first friend suggested that the word "Hatter" be deleted, because the sign already said "makes and sells hats." The next friend suggested deleting "makes and," because as long as the hats were well made, no one would care who made them. Another friend suggested deleting "for ready money," since in those days before credit cards, people customarily paid cash. Yet another friend suggested deleting "sells hats," since no one expected him to give away the hats. After all these suggestions were taken into account, the only things that remained to the sign were the name "John Thompson" and the picture of a hat. After hearing and laughing at the story, the delegates of the Continental Congress became satisfied with many fewer changes to the Declaration of Independence than they had proposed.[120]

• Thomas E. Dewey got into trouble early during his Presidential campaign against Harry Truman. On a cross-country journey by train, Mr. Dewey criticized the train engineer for leaving a station late. This caused much bad publicity for him, and *New York Times* reporter James Reston ended his article about the incident with "... and the train pulled off with a jerk."[121]

• Winston Churchill was a master of the English language, winning the Nobel Prize for Literature in 1953. Once he ran into a person who refused to end a sentence with a preposition, despite the unnatural sentences that resulted from his devotion to this rule. Sir Winston told the person, "This is English up with which I will not put."[122]

• A grandmother went to see Eve Ensler's *Vagina Monologues* with some family and friends. After the performance, she told her granddaughter, "Honey, next time I get together with my lady friends, we are going to talk about our vaginas. And if they say WHAT are you talking about? I'm going to say C*NT! C*NT!"[123]

• Yogi Berra once showed Phil Rizzuto through his new home. Mr. Rizzuto complimented him by saying, "Wow, Yogi! What a beautiful mansion you've got here!" "What do you mean, Phil?" Yogi asked. "It's nothing but a bunch of rooms."[124]

Letters

• Some fans are obsessive. One such fan assaulted a radio deejay because he would not constantly play her favorite Elvis songs. He found an innovative way to get back at her. He stuffed himself with pizza, carrots, candy, and wine, and then he vomited into a plastic bag. To the vomit he added an assortment of pills. Then he mailed the mess to the fan along with a letter saying that the National Elvis Fan Club wanted to give her "Elvis' Last Supper."[125]

• At one time, a rumor stated that President John Adams had sent General C.C. Pinckney to France so that he could pick out two French girls for himself and two for President Adams. In a letter to William Tudor, President Adams joked about the rumor, "If this be true, General Pinckney has kept them all for himself and cheated me out of my two."[126]

• Journalist George Jean Nathan of the *American Mercury* used to receive 200 hate letters a day — he paid attention only to the ones that were well written.[127]

Media

• After "Shoeless Joe" Jackson was thrown out of professional baseball because he was accused of helping to throw the 1919 World Series — despite batting .375 in the series — he received a telephone call from a radio show called *We the People*. The producer of the show wanted Mr. Jackson to come to New York and be interviewed. When Mr. Jackson asked how much money he would receive, he learned that he would earn no money, but be given only transportation and a hotel room. Mr. Jackson said, "You paid Lou Gehrig $5,000 to speak on your program not long ago. If Lou was worth that much to you, then I am, too" — and he hung up.[128]

• National League umpire Harry Wendelsted made a mistake as a rookie umpire in the Georgia-Florida League when he first ordered his uniform — he didn't order the extra room in the seat that allowed for comfortable crouching behind home plate. In fact, his pants were so tight that they split when he crouched behind home plate for the first game of the season. The next day, the Brunswick, Georgia newspaper carried a photograph of his rear end in his split pants under the headline: "Official Opening."[129]

• Early in the careers of ice dancers Jayne Torvill and Christopher Dean, members of the media thought that they were romantically involved because of the romantic programs they performed on the ice, so the media constantly asked them, "When are you getting married?" Through necessity, they developed responses to keep the media at bay: "Not yet" and "Not this week." (Eventually, they did get married — but not to each other.)[130]

• On the *Today* show, Peter Townsend, a former fiancé of Princess Margaret, was interviewed by Barbara Walters, who of course asked about his recent break-up with the Princess. He replied that he was tired of answering questions about it. Ms. Walters asked, "Well, if you're sick of talking about it, why is it in all your publicity releases?"[131]

• Shakespearean actress Julia Marlowe insisted on protecting her privacy. A syndicated columnist once tried to get her to say something by pointing out that what she said to him would be printed in 117 newspapers throughout the United States. She replied, "That is 117 reasons for not saying it."[132]

• Harry Hershfield made it a practice to always stand on the news photographer's left for group photographs — that way, his name appeared first in the newspaper caption.[133]

Mishaps

• Mishaps occur in nursing. When Joanne Murnane was a new nurse working in a hospital, one of her patients died. She prepared the dead patient, and seeing dentures on the dead patient's table, she stuffed the dentures in the dead patient's mouth and then took him to the hospital morgue. When she returned to the room to care for the other, live patient there, the live patient said, "Miss, have you seen my teeth? I laid them on this table but can't find them now." Of course, he had put his dentures on the wrong table. Thinking quickly, Nurse Murnane said, "I'm cleaning them for you, sir. I'll have them back soon." She says, "Of course, I did clean and sterilize the dentures and returned them to their correct owner, all the while thanking my lucky stars that all had worked out acceptably.[134]

• The famous can be mistaken for the unfamous. Charles Hanson Towne, a poet and the editor of *McClure's Magazine*, had long wanted to meet an actress, Mrs. Minnie Fiske, who was famous in the early 20th century. One day, he had his chance. She was playing at a benefit, and as she stepped off the stage into the wings, he was waiting for her. Mr. Towne poured out his admiration for her, and when he had finished, Mrs. Fiske tapped him on the arm with her lorgnette, smiled at him, and said, "Thank you, Mr. Electrician," and left.[135]

• Having experience as a soldier can be bad for a baseball player. A Los Angeles player named Ken Hicks began to pitch a game shortly after ending his term of service with the United States Army. He was beginning a pitch when the loudspeaker came to life with the words, "Attention, please!" Mr. Hicks assumed the proper military posture after hearing the word "attention," the umpire called a balk, and the runner on first advanced to second.[136]

• During an open-air performance of *Macbeth* starring Charlton Heston, arrangements were made for a dummy to be thrown into the ocean for Lady Macbeth's death. Unfortunately, during one performance the wind was blowing so heavily that when the dummy was thrown from a wall the wind blew the dummy back again — right at the feet of the actor who reported, "The queen is dead, my lord."[137]

• In a Victorian melodrama, Donald Wolfit played a cruel father who is stabbed to death by his own son in the last act. One day, the actor playing his son forgot the dagger. Not knowing what else to do, he kicked Mr. Wolfit in the seat of his pants. Seeking to save the play, Mr. Wolfit told the audience before his character died, "That boot! That boot! 'Twas poisoned!"[138]

• While Ralph Richardson was in military service during World War II, he sometimes had to handle very heavy books. The books contained secret information and were covered in lead so they could be sunk into the sea if need be — unfortunately, the books were located at Eastleigh, which is not on the ocean.[139]

Money

• Professional baseball player "Shoeless Joe" Jackson was nearly illiterate and seldom signed his name — his wife, Katie, had the task of signing his name to baseballs to meet the requests of fans. However, one paper he is known to have signed is his will. In the will, his and his wife's estate was given to the American Heart Association and the American Cancer Society. These charities would love to have the will so they can auction it off — it could bring in $100,000 — but the will has been ruled the property of the Probate Court.[140]

• Nemanja Petrovic, a 42-year-old beggar from Serbia, got tired of being ignored by passersby, so he threw his cap and shoes down on the street, wrote a sign that said, "Invisible Beggar," and then left for a while. When he got back, he got a nice surprise: "When I returned, I was astonished to find a crowd and my cap was full of money. Now I just put down the sign, a pair of shoes as a prop, and wait for the donations to roll in while I have a coffee over the road."[141]

• In 1942, professional golfer Sam Snead played two holes barefoot at the Masters in Augusta in order to help golf writer (and his personal manager) Fred Corcoran win a bet with his fellow sportswriters. (Mr. Snead birdied both holes!) By the way, Mr. Snead once paid out $2,000 in order to play in the British Open. He won the tournament — and earned $600.[142]

• Caroline Gall was a veterinarian who made a good salary, something that made many women envious of her in the 1970s. She once said, "If they would just go ahead and do something instead of bitching all the time. I run into housewives who will say, 'I wanted to be a vet, but I can't stand chemistry.' Well, I can't stand chemistry either, but I learned it." Well, I can't stand chemistry either, but I learned it." (This anecdote is applicable to many men as well.)[143]

• Before Ulysses S. Grant rose to a position of prominence, the union soldiers in the Civil War suffered from poor generalship. One day, President Abraham Lincoln learned that a Union brigadier general and 12 mules had been captured by Confederate soldiers. President Lincoln remarked, "How unfortunate! Those mules cost $200 apiece."[144]

• An editorial in *Variety* once stated that the Marx Brothers could make $20,000 a week if they would work together again. Groucho wrote (what I hope is a minority opinion) *Variety*, "Apparently you are under the impression that the only thing that matters in this world is money. That is quite true."[145]

Mothers

• In 2010, Kate Ogg gave birth to premature twins in Australia. Because they were born after just 27 weeks of pregnancy, a real chance of death existed. Daughter Emily did well following the birth, but son Jamie was not breathing. After 20 minutes of trying to get him to breathe, medical personnel pronounced him dead. Parents David and Kate Ogg wanted to get to know their son, so nurses placed him on her bare chest. Kate said, "I wanted to meet him and to hold him and for him to know us. If he was on his way out of the world, we wanted for him to know who his parents were and to know that we loved him before he died." But after about five minutes, Jamie began to move. Kate said, "We'd resigned ourselves to the fact we were going to lose him; we were just trying to make the most of those last precious moments." However, the doctor thought that Jamie was still dead and that his movements were the involuntary reflexes of a recently dead person. Soon, Jamie opened his eyes. Kate said, "We thought, 'What a blessing — we get to see his eyes before he passes away. But they stayed open!" David said, "I think half of us said [then], 'What if he actually makes it?' If he does, this would just be a miracle. The other half was saying, 'No, he's been declared dead, this is purely instinct.'" Jamie kept moving. He grabbed his mother's finger, and then he grabbed his father's finger. Kate put a drop of breast milk on her finger, and Jamie sucked it. Kate said, "We thought, 'He's getting stronger — he's not dead.'" The doctor, who was not present to observe Jamie's actions, still thought that Jamie's movements were mere reflex. Eventually, the doctor returned and listened to Jamie' heartbeat. Kate said, "He got a stethoscope, listened to Jamie's chest and just kept shaking his head. He said, 'I don't believe it, I don't believe it.'" Australians call holding an infant against its mother, skin to skin, kangaroo care — it is like the baby kangaroo being warm and protected in its mother's pouch. Kate said that the baby "comes out of you, and all of a sudden there isn't the warmth or smell of the mother or the sound of their heartbeat. And so putting him back on my chest was as close to him being inside me where he was safe." Dr. Lisa Eiland of the Weill Cornell Medical Center in New York City told NBC News, "What's important is the warmth that the mother provides and the stimulation that the baby may have received from hearing the mother's heartbeat. So those are all things that may have helped the baby in terms of going down the path to living as opposed to the path of death." David called Kate a "very strong, very smart wife." He added, "She instinctively did what she did. If she hadn't have done that, then Jamie probably wouldn't be here." When Jamie was a healthy five-month-old baby, he and the other members of the Ogg family appeared on *The Today Show*.[146]

• Tipper Gore was out driving with her daughters when they saw a dirty homeless woman muttering to herself on a street corner. Her daughters asked if they could take the homeless woman home with them, but Tipper gave reasons why they couldn't, then she and her daughters started to do volunteer work to help the homeless and to help the mentally ill. By the way, Tipper was named Mary Elizabeth Aitcheson at birth, but she received the nickname "Tipper" from a lullaby that her mother used to sing to her. Also by the way, Al Gore decided to become a politician in 1976. He was so nervous on the day that he announced his candidacy to become a representative from Tennessee that he vomited in a men's room.[147]

• Frith Banbury rapidly became a leading actor because of his mother, who was hard of hearing. When Mr. Banbury first started as an actor, he had small roles, but his mother, of course, attended his performances. Being hard of hearing, she cupped her ear and leaned forward whenever her son was on stage. Other audience members noticed this, and they paid special attention to her son, thinking that he must have important dialogue to impart. The play VIPs noticed the audience paying special attention to Mr. Banbury, and they rapidly made him a star.[148]

Names

• In some parts of the world, girls are not prized as highly as boys. For example, in India, girls are sometimes unwanted because providing dowries and paying for weddings for them is very expensive. Boys, on the other hand, are valued because when they get married, they receive a dowry and bring money into the family. In India, many girls have been given the names "Nakusa" or "Nakushi." In Hindi, these names mean "Unwanted." In October 2011, hundreds of girls in central India attended a renaming ceremony in which they shed their unwanted names and instead chose new names for themselves. Their new, self-chosen names include "Aishwarya" after a Bollywood star; "Savitri" after a Hindi goddess; and "Vaishali," which in Hindi means "prosperous, beautiful, and good." A 15-year-old girl who had shed her old name of "Nakusa" for her new name of "Ashmita," which in Hindi means "very tough," said, "Now in school, my classmates and friends will be calling me this new name, and that makes me very happy."[149]

• When Cassius Clay converted to Islam, he changed his name to Muhammad Ali. His new name means "someone who is worthy of praise." After taking his new name, Mr. Ali let it be known that he no longer wished to be called by his "slave name" — the name "Clay" had come from the owner of Mr. Ali's great-grandfather. Some of his opponents in the boxing ring continued to call him Cassius Clay. Mr. Ali responded by hitting them harder.[150]

• A supporter of General Lewis Cass, an ardent Democrat, proposed to name a Western county "Cass" in honor of the General, but one of the opponents of the Democrats moved that the first letter of the name "Cass" be stricken out. However, the General's supporter replied that it was unusual for a member of Congress to propose that a county be named after himself.[151]

Chapter 4: From Olympic Games to Religion

Olympic Games

• Figure skater Paul Wylie was known for a long time as a skater who performed best in practice, but in 1992 he won a silver medal at the Olympic Games. Afterward, reporters asked him if he thought he should have been awarded the gold medal, but Mr. Wylie replied, "How great of a Cinderella story do you guys want?"[152]

• At the 1992 Olympic Games in Barcelona, gymnast Shannon Miller won five medals, all silver or bronze. A reporter asked Ms. Miller if she were willing to trade her five silver and bronze medals for one gold medal. Her response? A very definite no. In the 1996 Olympics, she won gold.[153]

Physicians

• Harold Smithson was a well-loved medical doctor. Sharon Lucas, a Registered Nurse in Minnesota, tells two stories about him: 1) While playing Little League baseball, a boy had suffered a cut that required stitches. He had been given a local anesthetic and was lying on a gurney, and he could not see his arm. Dr. Smithson came in and started talking to him about baseball, and the conversation grew animated. Eventually, the boy asked, "Doctor, aren't you going to sew up my arm or something?" Dr. Smithson said, "Son, I've been sewing it up. In fact, it's all done as soon as I cut off the end of this thread." The boy had not felt anything. 2) Some patients are obnoxious, and this patient cursed his nurses while they worked on him in the emergency room. Dr. Smithson appeared and watched quietly, and the obnoxious patient yelled at him, "What the h*ll do you want?" Dr. Smithson replied, "At the moment I'd like to see your rear end leaving the emergency room." The patient yelled, "You can kiss my *ss." Dr. Smithson replied, "Son, this is not the time to get romantic."[154]

Politics

• A group of Soviet Communists visited the United States and toured a USAmerican car factory which had a parking lot filled with cars. The Communists were informed that the factory belonged to Henry Ford but that the cars in the parking lot were owned by the workers. Later, a group of USAmerican Capitalists visited the USSR, where they toured a car factory that had a parking lot with only one car in it. The Capitalists were informed that the factory belonged to the workers but that the car was owned by the factory manager.[155]

• Senator Warren Magnuson, a Democrat from Washington, had the nickname "Maggie." At a dinner with President Franklin D. Roosevelt, he was referred to as "Maggie" constantly. Winston Churchill asked Senator Magnuson about the nickname, then told him, "Young man, if I were you, I wouldn't resent it. I really think the reason that I'm Prime Minister of England is I'm known as Winnie in every pub in the country." After speaking with Sir Winston, Senator Magnuson never worried about his nickname.[156]

• Benjamin Disraeli often was forced to deal with hecklers. One person shouted, in an attempt to disrupt his speech, "Speak up! I can't hear you." Mr. Disraeli responded, "Truth travels slowly, but it will reach even you in time." On another occasion, someone shouted that Disraeli's rich wife had picked him out of the gutter. Mr. Disraeli responded, "My good fellow, if you were in the gutter, no one would pick you out."[157]

• In 1963, Adlai Stevenson went to Dallas, where a group of far-right extremists confronted him. Afterward, he said, "A woman hit me on the head with a placard, and a man hit me on the cheek with a different weapon. ... I asked the angry police not to prefer charges against them, not to punish them; after all, I didn't want them to go to jail — I thought it would be better if they went to school."[158]

• In the 1920s, politician Al Rabinowitz concluded a rousing speech about why he should be elected, and then he asked for comments from the audience. A pushcart peddler stood and said, "Mr. Rabinowitz, if you and I would campaign together all over New York, we could tell more lies than any other two men, and I wouldn't have to open my mouth."[159]

• Margaret Trudeau, the wife of Pierre, Prime Minister of Canada, was a free spirit. Frequently, the smell of marijuana drifted from the windows of the Ottawa residence of the Prime Minister, and a local police officer once gave her a gift of incense in an attempt to disguise the smell of the marijuana smoke.[160]

• President Lyndon Baines Johnson once got out of a limousine and walked toward some helicopters in Vietnam. A young military attaché told President Johnson, "Sir, your helicopter is over there." President Johnson replied, "Son, they're all my helicopters."[161]

• In the good old days, Senator George Vest was making a speech when the gaslights went out. Senator Vest announced, "I shall continue my speech. However, when the last person gets ready to leave the hall, let me know and I'll stop."[162]

• Lady Bird Johnson was more of a feminist than she has been given credit for. Frequently, when her husband, President Lyndon Johnson, returned home, she would ask him, "What have you done for women today?"[163]

Practical Jokes

• Judi Dench's co-stars enjoy teasing her. While John Miller was researching his biography of her, he witnessed a fluff by Ms. Dench while she was acting in a TV series. Geoffrey Palmer told Mr. Miller loudly, so Judi would hear, "Make sure you put this in your book, John — she isn't always perfect!" On another occasion, Mr. Miller was talking with Billy Connolly, who also spoke loudly so she could hear, "Sssshh, she's coming — I'll finish telling you later." In addition, once when Ms. Dench was being interviewed, she laughed when she heard Mr. Connolly tease her by screaming in the next room, "She was a *nightmare* to work with."[164]

• In 1916, Casey Stengel bet Brooklyn Dodger manager Wilbert Robinson that he couldn't catch a baseball thrown out of an airplane. Wilbert accepted the bet, and Casey got an airplane with an open cockpit. As Wilbert stood in the field wearing a baseball mitt, Casey and the pilot flew over the field. At this time, one of the greatest practical jokes in baseball occurred. Casey didn't throw a baseball from the plane — he threw a grapefruit which splattered all over Wilbert's chest. Wilbert was so angry that Casey was forced to stay in hiding until he was forgiven.[165]

• Sports columnist Fred Russell of the *Nashville Banner* made lots of telephone calls in his business. Whenever he heard that a VIP was out and therefore unavailable to talk, he would say something like, "This is Mr. Haynes at the Cameo Pool Hall [pool halls were then regarded as disreputable places]. He left his cap over here last night. Just tell him I'll take good care of it and he can get it tomorrow night."[166]

• Members of the Benson Company, a traveling Shakespearean troupe, often played practical jokes on newcomers to the company. Once, a newcomer arrived at the train station wearing a kilt because the company was crossing the border into Scotland that day, and he had been told that it was a tradition that members of the Benson Company wore a kilt whenever they traveled into Scotland.[167]

• Baseball player Bob Uecker was on an airplane when the intercom mike at the back was left unguarded. Mr. Uecker picked it up and said, "This is your captain speaking. Please remain seated and keep your safety belts fastened until the plane has hit the side of the terminal building and come to a stop."[168]

Prayer

• A farmer and his wife — who were childless — came to the Hasidic leader known as the Maggid of Mezeritch and pleaded with him to pray to God to allow them to have a child. The Maggid agreed, but he believed that such a prayer should come from the farmer and his wife, so he named a high price for his services. The farmer tried to bargain with him, but the Maggid refused, saying that the farmer and his wife must pay the full price. Finally, the farmer turned to his wife and said, "Let's go home and pray to God by ourselves. God will help us for free." After the farmer and his wife had left, the Maggid smiled.[169]

• R' Levi Yitzchak of Berdichev once prayed to God on a Rosh Hashanah that fell on the Sabbath that He must write the names of all human beings in the Book of Life. Why? Since writing is forbidden on the Sabbath, God cannot write names in the Book of Death. However, God can write names in the Book of Life because when there is danger to human life (*piku'ach nefesh*), then writing is permitted on the Sabbath to save those lives.[170]

Prejudice

• Lots of people know that Jackie Robinson broke the color line barring blacks from playing in major-league baseball, but they don't know that he broke the color line barring black baseball players from dining in restaurants — even in northern cities. For a long time — even after black and white professional baseball players started staying at the same hotels — the black players wouldn't eat in the hotel dining rooms and would instead order room service. One day, Mr. Robinson walked into a dining room in a Cincinnati hotel. The headwaiter showed him to a seat, a waiter gave him a menu and took his order, Mr. Robinson ate his meal, none of the other diners walked out in high dungeon, and the sky did not fall. After that, other black baseball players started eating in hotel dining rooms.[171]

• Adolf Hitler felt that the 1936 Olympic Games in Germany would show the superiority of white Aryans over other human beings, such as blacks. Instead, African-American runner Jesse Owens became the star of the Olympics and non-Aryans won most of the medals. Hitler would have disapproved of the friendship that sprang up between Mr. Owens and white German long jumper Luz Long. Mr. Long even gave Mr. Owens good advice that helped him to reach the finals of the long jump.[172]

• Ralph Bunche, the first African-American to win the Nobel Peace Prize, was raised by his grandmother, Nana, a light-skinned woman. In Los Angeles, when Ralph was young, a cemetery plot salesman came to their house and talked to Nana. The salesman thought that Nana was white, so he assured her that no blacks or Mexicans would be buried near the cemetery plot. Nana grabbed a broom and chased the salesman away.[173]

• When segregation was still a big part of the USAmerican scene, Jewish comedian George Jessel took black singer Lena Horne to the Stork Club. The headwaiter pretended not to be able to find a reservation and finally asked, "Mr. Jessel, who made the reservation?" Mr. Jessel replied, "Abraham Lincoln."[174]

• A hospital orderly once took care of a truly racist patient. The orderly gave the man a sponge bath with a chemical that turns white skin black for several days. A nurse in on the joke told the racist that blood from a black person had been used in his most recent transfusion. Unfortunately, the racist stayed racist.[175]

Problem-Solving

• In 2009, Roger Ebert and his wife, Chaz, attended the Cannes Film Festival, where credentials are expensive but are usually necessary to see movies. A man named Scott Collette, who faithfully read Roger's essays on the WWW, emailed him: "I am currently in Cannes, working out of an office on the Croisette across from the Palais. Work ends Tuesday/Wednesday and I am here until the end of the festival and I am very worried that when all is said and done, I will have attended the largest film festival in the world and will have not seen any films." Roger suggested that Scott do what Raven, Roger's granddaughter, was doing: Going to the movie theater and holding up a sign begging for a ticket (*Invitation, si'l vous plait!*). After leaving a movie theater fresh from seeing *Map of the Sounds of Tokyo*, Roger and Chaz ran into Scott, who proudly held up a precious movie ticket and said, "I got in!" Roger asked him what he had done to get the ticket. Scott replied, "What Raven did — I begged."[176]

• Gene Fowler occasionally suffered from headaches while working as a screenwriter at MGM, but he didn't have anywhere to lie down because an efficiency expert had ordered all the sofas removed from writers' offices. This made Mr. Fowler mad, so he told the efficiency expert that unless he had a sofa by 4 p.m., he was going to throw all the furniture he could find outside his office window, then set fire to the studio backlot and its many expensive sets. The efficiency expert laughed at him, and at 4 p.m., Mr. Fowler began to throw all his furniture out his office window. After throwing out all his own furniture, he began to throw out furniture from other offices. Of course, MGM tried to stop him, but Mr. Fowler and his confederates had locked all the doors. After an hour of mayhem, a truck arrived, bearing a new couch for Mr. Fowler, and peace was declared.[177]

• Educators tend to be creative problem-solvers. For example, a number of schools in England had problems with girls wearing skirts that were much too short and violated the schools' dress codes. Teachers were spending too much time enforcing the dress code, and they wanted to spend more time teaching. They solved the problem of too-short skirts by banning skirts altogether. Now girls as well as boys have to wear trousers. Publicly funded Nailsea School is one school that banned skirts. Headmaster David New says about the dress-code violations that resulted in the ban, "We didn't want to waste any more time on it. [The ban] just means that teachers can concentrate on what's important in education."[178]

• As an Impressionist painter, Claude Monet was obsessed with recreating the effect of light on various objects. In 1890, he began painting a picture of *meules* — stacks of wheat or oats. The light changed suddenly, so he got another canvas and began painting the effect of that light on the *meules*. Again, the light changed, and again, he got another canvas and began painting the effect of that new light on the *meules*. After this experience, he started to always paint on more than one canvas. As the light changed, he switched to a different canvas. This allowed him to keep on working whether the day was sunny or cloudy, and when the day was sunny in the morning and cloudy in the afternoon.[179]

• Before baseball had modern stadiums, some people always watched the games for free by standing in back of the outfield. In Boston in 1884, the club's owner decided to put up fences to prevent freeloaders from seeing the games; however, many freeloaders simply climbed the telegraph poles and watched the games from their high perch. This made the owner angry, so he waited until the middle of an exciting game, then sent out crews to paint several feet of the telegraph poles — from the ground to the freeloaders. All of the freeloaders ruined their clothing getting down from the telegraph poles.[180]

• During her rule, Queen Mary I of England persecuted the Protestants. Benjamin Franklin's great-great-grandfather was a Protestant under her rule, but he continued to read the Bible even when doing so was forbidden. He kept the Bible strapped underneath a covered stool, and when he wanted to read it, he stationed one of his children to serve as a lookout, then he turned the stool over. Whenever the child said that an officer of the crown was coming near, Benjamin Franklin's great-great-grandfather would immediately hide the evidence of his Bible reading by turning the stool right-side up.[181]

• Occasionally an actor forgets his lines. Once an actor was on stage when he forgot his lines while playing a king who was supposed to roar out his orders at another character. Instead of roaring out his orders, he motioned for the other character to come close to him, then whispered to him that he couldn't remember his part. Then, when the other character walked away from him, the actor said loudly, "Forget nothing that I have told you." The audience was completely unaware that the actor had forgotten his lines.[182]

• This is an example of underground political humor from the time when Lithuania suffered from Russian rule: A Lithuanian in the days of Communist domination had a never-ending supply of fresh fruits and vegetables. A visitor marveled at this plenitude and asked the Lithuanian how he managed it. "It's easy," he said. "I have a parrot which I taught to say pro-Communist slogans. I take the parrot to the market, and when it squawks, 'Long live Communism,' everyone throws fruits and vegetables at it."[183]

• During Prohibition, bootleggers used to smuggle small boatloads of alcohol into the United States. If federal agents were about to apprehend them, the bootleggers would throw the alcohol overboard to get rid of the incriminating evidence. Often, the illegal alcohol was weighted down with salt to sink it. When the salt dissolved long after the federal agents had gone, a small buoy was released to float on the surface of the water and let the bootleggers know exactly where to find the alcohol.[184]

• Heinie Zimmerman, who played third base for the Chicago Cubs early in this century, hated umpires. In 1913, he received an interesting letter in the mail. The letter contained half of a $100 bill and a note saying that he would receive the other half if he would quit verbally abusing umpires for two weeks. Mr. Zimmerman managed to restrain himself, and after the two weeks was up, an umpire gave him the other half of the $100 bill.[185]

• At age 16, Jessica Hopper started a band that opened for DIY band Fugazi in the Twin Cities. This was a highly coveted gig, and many, many Twin Cities bands had telephoned the club's booker to ask to be the opening band. How did Jessica's band get the opening slot? Simple. She telephoned Fugazi directly. She says, "It worked — and p*ssed off every other band in town because we were terrible."[186]

• A master carpenter had a job open, and an apprentice approached him for it. The master carpenter asked, "Have you ever made a mistake?" The young apprentice replied, "No," thinking that his answer would get him the job. However, the master carpenter told him, "There is no way that I am going to hire you because when you do make a mistake, you won't know how to fix it."[187]

• Until 1954, when he was drafted, New York Yankee Billy Martin, a small man, wore No. 12. During his military service, No. 1 became available, and it was waiting for him when he returned to professional baseball. According to Mr. Martin, the Yankee clubhouse manager had saved the number for him: "He said my back wasn't big enough for two numbers."[188]

• While traveling by train, the great actress Sarah Bernhardt was annoyed by a German officer who would neither quit smoking nor allow her to open the window. Therefore, to breathe clean air she smashed her elbow against the window and broke it.[189]

Profanity

• Harry S. Truman occasionally used profanity, something that Richard "Expletive Deleted" Nixon tried to make a campaign issue when he ran for President against John F. Kennedy. Mr. Kennedy responded, "I would not want to give the impression that I am taking former President Truman's use of language lightly. I have sent him the following wire: 'Dear Mr. President: I have noted with interest your suggestion as to where my opponent should go. While I understand and sympathize with your deep motivation, I think it important that our side try to refrain from raising the religious issue.'"[190]

• President Abraham Lincoln once reviewed the first corps of the army. Being driven to the place of review by an ambulance composed of a wagon and a team of six mules, President Lincoln listened for a while as the driver cursed his six mules, then he asked the man, "Are you an Episcopalian?" Startled, the mule-driver replied, "No, Mr. President, I am a Methodist." President Lincoln then said, "I thought you must be an Episcopalian, because you swear just like Governor Seward, who is a church warden."[191]

• Umpire Augie Donatelli was the only umpire ever to throw Bobby Thompson out of a game. Later, Mr. Thompson asked Mr. Donatelli why he had done that. Mr. Donatelli explained that he had been forced to do it — Mr. Thompson had called him a #$%^&*. "That's right," said Mr. Thompson, "but why did you throw me out for that? No one heard it but you and me and the catcher." "I know, Bobby," said Mr. Donatelli, "but I didn't want that catcher going through life thinking I was a #$%^&*."[192]

• The men soccer referees in Derby, England decided that they didn't want to officiate the games of the women soccer players, so in 1973 they started teaching women to be referees. Why? Because the language of the women soccer players was too strong for the male referees; as an official explained, "Although the ladies' keenness is commendable, [male] referees who officiate at their matches rarely want to do so again. ... The language can be quite startling."[193]

• Umpire Eric Gregg was bilingual, and sometimes he tried to help Spanish-speaking baseball players with their English. Once, catcher Tony Peña asked him, "Where the h*ll was that pitch at?" Mr. Gregg replied, "Tony, you can't end a sentence with a preposition. You can't end a sentence with 'at.'" Mr. Peña was a quick learner. He said, "OK, where the h*ll was that pitch at, *ssh*le?"[194]

• As a young man, Jerome K. Jerome (1859-1927) acted in England. He and the other actors tended to swear, and in an attempt to break the habit, they decided to fine themselves a penny for each swear word they uttered. Unfortunately, they were forced to stop the attempt against swearing — within two hours, Mr. Jerome and the other actors were broke.[195]

• Babe Ruth got into trouble when he was a boy, and so he had to go to St. Mary's Industrial School for Boys. When he grew up, he wanted other kids to avoid the mistakes he had made, so if he ever heard any children using profanity, he would yell at them, "Godd*mn it, stop that godd*mn swearing over there."[196]

Public Speaking

• In 1951, Robert F. Kennedy invited Ralph Bunche, the first African-American to win the Nobel Peace Prize, to speak at a legal forum at the University of Virginia. Mr. Bunche wrote back that he was willing to speak, but only before an integrated audience. At that time, many University of Virginia students objected to black people and white people being seated together. Mr. Kennedy made a great effort and persuaded the students to allow integration, and Mr. Bunche spoke before an audience in which black people and white people were seated together.[197]

• The Maggid of Slutzk, R' Zvi Dainov was known for giving the same speech over and over again, though in different locations. When he was asked why he did this, he replied, "The doctor does the same thing. He writes a prescription for one patient, and writes the exact same prescription for another suffering from the same disease."[198]

Religion

• In my opinion, even people who believe in the one true God should be allowed to poke fun at Him. (I hope that God has a sense of humor.) Once a man went to a tailor and ordered a pair of pants. Week after week, the man came back, but the tailor said the pants weren't ready. After a month had gone by, the tailor finally said the pants were ready. The man put on the pants and was very pleased because they fit perfectly. However, as he paid for the pants, he said, "God made the World in only six days, yet you took an entire month to make these pants." "That's true," replied the tailor. "But look at the quality of those pants, and compare them to the shape the World's in."[199]

• An angel showed a new arrival around Heaven. Coming to a high wall, the angel put a finger to his lips and said, "Shh! Behind this wall are the fundamentalists. They think they are the only ones in Heaven."[200]

Chapter 5: From Royalty to Work

Royalty

• In 1960, Senator John Sparkman, a Democrat from Alabama, was introduced to the Queen of Greece. He introduced himself as "Senator John Sparkman," but a colleague told him he should have added the rest — "Senator John Sparkman *of Alabama*." The Queen overheard and asked, "Oh, are you from Alabama?" After the Senator admitted that he was, the Queen said that she had met a young lieutenant recently, who had told her, "I'm from Alabama, honey." Senator Sparkman said that the lieutenant should have added the rest — "I'm from Alabama, honey *child*." For the rest of evening, everybody called the Queen of Greece "Honey Child."[201]

• In 1955, Illinois Governor Adlai Stevenson had dinner with Princess Margaret. As he talked to her, he noticed that he had gravy on his hand, so he reached under the table for a napkin and began to wipe away the gravy. Princess Margaret (who had a sense of humor) stared at him, then said, "Governor Stevenson, will you kindly remove your filthy hand from my scarf?"[202]

Signs

• When Hurricane Irene hit the USAmerican east coast in August 2011, some people responded with wit. For example, the Hieronymous Seafood Restaurant and Oyster Bar in Wilmington, NC has an outdoor sign on which it can post messages by using individual, physical letters rather than letters formed by light bulbs or light-emitting diodes. This is the message that the restaurant posted: "We are open until the letters fly off this sign." Another restaurant posted this sign: "Irene, You Have No Reservation."[203]

• Harry Ackerman used to display this sign in his restaurant: "COURTEOUS, EFFICIENT SELF-SERVICE."[204]

Success

• Some people are driven to be successful because they were unpopular in school — especially, I think, in high school. Mike Nichols, of course, was a successful comedian with Elaine May, and he became a successful director. Once, someone came up to him and said, "You don't remember me, but — ." Mr. Nichols replied, "I remember you very well. You're Eddie Pompadour. You're a prick." Eddie had bullied Mr. Nichols when they were kids. Mr. Nichols asked Eddie, "So, what are you doing now?" Eddie said, "I'm selling used cars." Mr. Nichols said, "I'm *so* glad."[205]

• Soccer superstar Julie Foudy has worn No. 11 ever since she was in the 6th grade, when she chose it because "I figured it meant I was double No. 1."[206]

Sports

• Tom Danehy, columnist for *Tucson Weekly* in Tucson, Arizona, is also a coach in many sports. For example, he coaches middle school six-man flag football during the late summer and early fall. In 2011, his star player was Hope, a left-handed Asian girl. About Hope, Mr. Danehy says, "In probably half the games this season, she was clearly the best athlete on the field for either team." Having a girl on the team doesn't bother the other players, but some adults are puzzled and one asked Mr. Danehy, "So, what are you trying to prove? Is this some kind of social experiment?" He replied, "Dude, your kid's team just got whupped, and that 'social experiment' accounted for four touchdowns." (Hope returned an interception for a touchdown, passed for a touchdown, and ran for two touchdowns.)[207]

• Goalies in professional ice hockey often wear No. 1 on their uniforms. The custom goes back to the days when teams traveled by train to play away games. Because the teams had to travel so far, the players slept in berths — small sleeping compartments stacked one on top of another. The lower berths were more comfortable for sleeping (and more convenient to get in and out of), so they were greatly desired. Teams decided to award sleeping berths on the basis of the numbers the players wore because in those days the players with the most seniority had the lowest numbers. However, teams gave the lowest number of all — No. 1 — to goalies because being a goalie is rugged work and goalies are usually exhausted after a game.[208]

• Gymnastics can be dangerous. Indiana State gymnast Kurt Thomas and several other members of his and Oklahoma University's men's gymnastics team once watched the women's gymnastics teams suffer through a very bad meet — with bodies flying everywhere — in Oklahoma City. Mr. Thomas had his jacket stuffed in his mouth as he watched, Bart Conner covered his eyes with his hands, and several men gymnasts left because the scene was so horrific and they were too scared to watch.[209]

• Figure skaters often have the reputation of being gay (not that there's anything wrong with that) — sometimes the reputation is deserved, but sometimes it is not. Young pairs figure skater Robert Davenport was teased at a skating camp by hockey players who told him, "All figure skaters are fags." Young Rob replied, "Look. You guys are in the locker room all by yourselves. You play hockey together while I'm surrounded by girls. Now who's the fag?"[210]

• The USSR was known for its men's singles skaters and its pairs skating teams, but it never produced a really fine women's singles skater until after its breakup. While the USSR was still together, pairs champion and coach Stanislav Zhuk was asked why. He joked, "Because I don't coach them."[211]

Theater

• On 27 December 1904, James M. Barrie's play, *Peter Pan*, opened. When Tinker Bell drank the poison, Peter Pan, played by Nina Boucicault, asked the audience to clap if they believed in fairies. This was an important moment in the play. If the audience clapped, the play would be a success; if they didn't, the play would fail. The audience clapped thunderously, and Ms. Boucicault burst into tears on stage. By the way, Mr. Barrie created the role of Tinker Bell in *Peter Pan* after he saw a small child wave his foot at a firefly. Also by the way, one actress whose name has remained on the programs for *Peter Pan* since the play debuted, is Jane Wren (sometimes Jenny Wren). She is listed as Tinker Bell, even though Tinker Bell is actually a spotlight reflected in a mirror — her voice is created by bells. Also by the way, *Peter Pan*, was (and is) amazingly successful and has provided some actors decades of work. The original Smee, George Shelton, played the part for 24 years. Bettering that record was William Luff, who played first Cecco and then Captain Hook for 45 years.[212]

• Director Max Reinhardt (1873-1943) was serious about his Shakespeare productions. In 1933, he created a production of *A Midsummer Night's Dream* for the Oxford University Dramatic Society. He looked over the countryside — it was an outdoor production — and then said, "Very nice, but [here he pointed at the village of Headington in the distance] that village over there must be removed." The effects he devised for the play were remarkable. At the beginning of the play, the actors simply stepped out from behind the trees where they had been hiding, and at one point Puck runs across the field, then vanishes — by jumping into a pit that was hidden from the audience.[213]

• To publicize a performance of Eve Ensler's *Vagina Monologues* at the University of California at Santa Cruz, the cast and crew put up such signs as "Have you made a clitoris happy today?" and "'What are we saying about our bodies if we can't say *vagina*?' — Eve Ensler." By the way, Tovah Feldmanstern wished to direct Eve Ensler's *Vagina Monologues* at her high school. Denied permission, she directed it outside of school. Also by the way, Ms. Ensler, writer and star of *The Vagina Monologues*, has had some interesting experiences. She was once served a salad made to look like a woman's exterior sexual anatomy — bean sprouts represented pubic hair.[214]

• William Schwenck Gilbert, a writer of genius as *H.M.S. Pinafore* and *The Pirates of Penzance* show, was occasionally very sharp as a director. An actor once told him, "Look here, sir, I will not be bullied. I know my lines." Mr. Gilbert replied, "That may be, but you don't know mine." By the way, Mr. Gilbert died a hero. On 29 May 1911, a woman swimming in his lake called out for help, and he helped her to reach land, but being 74 years old, he died as a result of his exertion.[215]

• Lennox Robinson, an Irish actor-manager, once auditioned a middle-aged woman who wished to be an actress. She spoke a few lines from the "quality of mercy" speech by Portia in Shakespeare's *Merchant of Venice*, then said, "I think I'd do better without me teeth," removed her teeth, and finished the speech. According to Mr. Robinson, "Auditions can sometimes be trying; one does not always discover genius."[216]

• Harley Granville-Barker was very sparing in giving praise as a theatrical director. When he was directing John Gielgud in *King Lear*, he would sometimes say, "You did some fine things today in that scene. I hope you know what they were." Then he would give Mr. Gielgud a long list of the things he had done wrong![217]

• Lilian Baylis' theatrical company was once invited to perform in the open air at Elsinore. Unfortunately, it rained and rained, and Ms. Baylis, who was always very concerned about her company, went to the door of her hotel, looked out at the rain, and then said indignantly, "This will have to stop."[218]

• While playing in the poor play *Alice's Boys*, Sir Ralph Richardson once went to the front of the stage and asked, "Is there a doctor in the house?" After a man stood up and identified himself as a doctor, Sir Ralph asked him, "Doctor, isn't this a terrible play?"[219]

Transplants

• As Christmas 2009 drew near, Dawn Pflughaupt, age 37, was happy because she was cancer-free. A bone marrow transplant with her brother, Brock Pflughaupt, as donor cured her leukemia. She had found out that she had leukemia after feeling ill. Dawn said, "I had bruises and was tired, but I thought that was from working in the automotive industry." She worked for Chrysler in Sedalia, MO. She went to the hospital and was at first diagnosed with a viral infection, but soon she received a telephone call. She said, "They told me I might bleed out if I didn't come to the hospital." That was when she learned that she had leukemia. One bad thing was that she had not spoken with most members of her family for over a decade, the result of some bad life choices that resulted in a prison term for her for selling marijuana. She said, "I was a good kid gone bad. I was on the wrong path, and I thought I was big, bad, tough, and strong." However, Brock, her brother, kept talking to her. She said, "He was always checking up on me, and he always let me know when there was a graduation or wedding." Her father had died in 2005, but the other members of her family rallied around her. Dawn said, "That was hard: Knowing I was sick and I never talked to him before he died." She began chemotherapy and radiation treatments. Her sister, Tara Wolfe, stayed by her side. Dawn said, "We rekindled our relationship, and Tara dropped everything to be with me." Tara volunteered to be a bone-marrow donor for Dawn, but she was not a match. Things were going badly for Dawn, who said, "It was rough and hard. I had no immune system, and I was crying blood and delusional." Brock then volunteered to be a bone-marrow donor for her. Dawn said, "Brock and I are like twins, as much as we look alike." He was a 99.98 percent match, the transplant took place, and it cured Dawn's leukemia. Before the transplant took place, Brock endured a series of injections that turned his platelets into white blood cells. Dawn said, "He was so stiff and sore. He was walking around like the Michelin Man." She added, "He's my hero." Dawn and Brock's mother, Jacqui, said, "I'm not one bit surprised by my son's actions. It's in his DNA." She added, "His father would be so proud." Brock said simply, "That's just what family does." Dawn is now cancer-free: "There are no words to describe how I feel. All I can do to thank Brock is appreciate life and live it to the fullest." The family members are now close. Jacqui said, "Families have ins and outs.

Sometimes God taps you on the shoulder, and sometimes He takes a baseball bat to the side of your head. We got the baseball bat." Brock registered for the National Bone Marrow Registry. He said about donating his bone marrow, "It hurt, but it won't deter me from donating again."[220]

• In 2007, Stephen Wilson gave his sister, Andrea, a gift that will help allow her to see her children, Andrew, age 12, and Laura, age 15, grow to adulthood: He gave her one of his kidneys. Both Stephen and Andrea are from Westerhope, Newcastle, England. Andrea, age 42, said, "I'm just so grateful. I am forever in his debt. He's given me a future with my children. We have always been close, but we have a special bond now." Twelve years previously, Andrea's kidneys were damaged during her second pregnancy when she suffered from pre-eclampsia. In 2006, her health began to rapidly fail. Andrea said, "The doctors said my kidneys were failing, and I was put on the waiting list for a transplant. They said the average wait in Newcastle was two years, but they had to find a kidney that was a perfect match and that could take much longer." Every night for eight hours, she was attached to a dialysis machine. She said, "It was really scary. I was getting worried that I wouldn't get one [a transplant]." Family members and friends volunteered to be tested, and Stephen turned out to be a perfect match. Andrea said, "He jumped at the chance to help me. I kept asking him if he was sure and saying he didn't have to, but he was determined to do it." She added, "If it hadn't been for Stephen, I could have waited years and years for a kidney. And the longer you are on dialysis, the more ill you get." Stephen said, "Having one kidney doesn't make me feel any different, but I think me and Andrea are closer now because we went through this together. I have sacrificed part of myself, but after seeing how ill Andrea was and how worried her children were, it's worth it." Andrea said, "I want people to be aware that there is a real shortage of kidneys. You never think about it until it happens to you. But it can happen to any one of us. I feel so lucky that Stephen was there to help me."[221]

Travel

• Irish playwright Brendan Behan spent time in prison, and he liked gallows humor. He used to tell a joke about a lawyer who boasted that he had gotten a client a suspended sentence — his client was hung. By the way, when traveling from Ireland through England to France, Mr. Behan was arrested by the British authorities, who deported him — to France, not Ireland, and they even paid his fare. Because of this, Mr. Behan once described the English as "a humorous and decent people."[222]

• Before the First World War, Alexander Woollcott was shocked by the speed of the taxicabs in Paris. He once asked his woman taxi driver, "Is there no speed limit in this city?" She replied sweetly, "Oh, yes, monsieur, but no one has succeeded in reaching it."[223]

Umpires

• Minor league umpire Scott Chestnut respected some baseball players. Once, some grit flew in his eye during a pitch so he couldn't see, so he asked the batter, "Red" Blume of the New Orleans team, whether it had been a ball or a strike. Red said it had been a ball, so Mr. Chestnut called it a ball. The catcher for Chattanooga was incredulous and asked why he had let Mr. Blume make the call. Mr. Chestnut replied, "Because I have always found Mr. Blume to be a man of high integrity." When the catcher said that he hoped that Mr. Chestnut would let him make some important calls, Mr. Chestnut replied, "I will, as soon as you prove to me you are half the man Mr. Blume is." The next pitch was a strike, and the New Orleans manager, Johnny Dobbs, complained about the call, saying that it was a foot outside. Mr. Dobbs turned to Mr. Blume for corroboration and asked, "Wasn't it outside, Red?" Mr. Blume replied, "No, Johnny, it was right down the middle."[224]

• Les Moss, a good man at repairing baseball gloves, once was given the glove of an opposing player, catcher Clint Courtney, to mend. He did so, but he also sewed some pieces of Limburger cheese into the glove. As the game wore on that day, the catcher's mitt began to stink. Umpire Ed Hurley noticed the stink, and he asked Mr. Courtney, "Don't you feel well?" Mr. Courtney said he felt fine, but the stink grew worse as the game continued, and eventually Umpire Hurley threw Mr. Courtney out of the game with a strict order to see a trainer about his "problem."[225]

• In the minor leagues, an umpire named Patrick Shaner grew tired of criticism from the fans, so during a game he walked away from the plate, went up to the stands, and took a seat. After the next pitch was thrown, he turned toward an abusive fan and asked, "What do you think it was — a ball or a strike?" The fan replied, "I can't tell — we're too far away." Umpire Shaner said, "You're right. Now I'll go back to my regular place of business." The fan remained quiet for the rest of the game.[226]

• In 1946, during a Red Sox game, umpire Red Jones began hearing insults coming from the Boston dugout. He threw two Red Sox players out of the game, but the same voice kept hurling insults at him, so he threw out five more Red Sox players. Still, the same voice hurled insults at him. Eventually, Mr. Jones threw everyone in the dugout out of the game — but the same voice kept insulting him. Later, he found out that a ventriloquist had been sitting behind the Red Sox dugout.[227]

• Baseball manager Ralph Houk enjoyed arguing with umpires. He once challenged rookie umpire Art Frantz in Mr. Frantz' very first game as a major league umpire. He told Mr. Frantz, "No bush-league SOB is going to throw me out of the game," and Mr. Frantz told him, "I'll see you tomorrow, Ralph."[228]

• After Babe Ruth had stuck out, he started arguing with umpire Babe Tinelli, saying, "There's 40,000 people here who know that last one was a ball, tomato head." Mr. Tinelli replied, "Maybe so, but mine is the only opinion that counts."[229]

War

• This is an example of underground political humor from the time when Lithuania suffered from Russian rule: A Lithuanian farmer once found an ancient lamp in a field. Because it was dirty, he rubbed it — and a genie appeared and granted him three wishes. The Lithuanian thought a moment about his wishes, then said, "My first wish is for China to invade Lithuania. My second wish is for China to invade Lithuania. My third wish is for China to invade Lithuania." The genie asked why the Lithuanian wanted China to invade Lithuania three times. The Lithuanian replied, "Because the Chinese Army will have to cross Russia six times."[230]

• While having dinner with President Abraham Lincoln, a man complained about how hard it would be to beat the Confederate soldiers in the Civil War: "You can't do anything with them Southern fellows. If they get whipped, they'll retreat to them Southern swamps and bayous along with the fishes and crocodiles. You haven't got the fish-nets made that'll catch them." President Abraham Lincoln listened to the man, and then said, "We've got just the nets for traitors, in the bayous or anywhere." "What kind of nets?" asked the man. President Lincoln replied, "Bayou-nets," and speared a fishball with his fork.[231]

• Many soldiers in South Vietnam were killed by North Vietnamese snipers. While in Vietnam, Colin Powell suggested to Captain Vo Cong Hieu that his soldiers wear bulletproof vests, but Captain Hieu wasn't convinced that they would help. But on patrol a soldier wearing a bulletproof vest was hit by a sniper's bullet that knocked him down. The man stood up, and Mr. Powell removed the flattened bullet from the vest and showed it to the other soldiers. After that vivid demonstration, more soldiers began to wear bulletproof vests.[232]

• An Army doctor had a crisis of conscience because it seemed that every time he succeeded in healing a wounded soldier, the soldier would go back into battle only to get killed. Therefore, the doctor left the Army and studied with a Zen master. The study worked, and the doctor returned to the Army. Thereafter, whenever he had doubts about why he was healing soldiers, he told himself, "Because I'm a doctor."[233]

• Major Alexis Casdagli found an interesting way of defying the Nazis while he was in a World War II prisoner-of-war camp: He did needlework. He created a cross-stitch sampler that had a border of dots and dashes that were messages in Morse code. What were the messages? "God save the King" and "F**k Hitler." Many Nazis saw the sampler, but none deciphered the Morse code messages.[234]

• General George B. McClellan felt that President Abraham Lincoln was interfering when he requested to be kept better informed of activities in the field. Therefore, the general sent the president this sarcastic telegram: "HAVE JUST CAPTURED SIX COWS. WHAT SHALL WE DO WITH THEM?" President Lincoln was able to meet the challenge. He sent back this telegram: "MILK THEM."[235]

• At a meeting of delegates, a politician made the motion that the standing army of the United States ought to consist of no more than 5,000 soldiers. George Washington whispered to the delegate from Maryland that in that case, he ought to amend the motion by providing that no enemy could invade the United States with an army of more than 3,000 soldiers.[236]

• Ernest Thesiger, an actor, enjoyed needlework, and during World War I he was popular with the other soldiers, who enjoyed seeing him sitting in the trenches, his hands busy with his needlework. He was a good soldier, and after the war he did his needlework with hands that were scarred from shrapnel.[237]

• A very young Catholic girl was shown around a Protestant Church in which a service flag was hung. She asked what the flag was, and she was informed that the flag was hung in honor of those who died in the service. She asked, "The 9:30 a.m. service or the 11 a.m. service?"[238]

• During his tour of America, Oscar Wilde noted that many Southerners date events by the Civil War. He once said that he had mentioned how lovely the moonlight was to a Southerner, and the Southerner replied, "Yes, but you should have seen it before the war."[239]

Work

• Mildred Burke, aka Mildred the Great, was an early pro wrestler of the 1930s through 1950s. Sometimes, she wrestled men, and in approximately 200 matches against men, she lost only once. She had lifted the challenger over her head and was throwing him to the ground when his knee hit her head and knocked her out. Often, she slept in her car as she traveled from match to match, but in 1938, she made $50,000 — that year, major-league baseball players were averaging $6,000. By the way, Lillian Ellison is known in pro wrestling circles as the Fabulous Moolah. In the late 1940s, she met promoter Jack Pfefer, who asked her why she wanted to get into wrestling. She answered, "For the moolah." "Moolah" means "money," and Mr. Pfefer gave Ms. Ellison the name of the Fabulous Moolah.[240]

• Major league baseball umpire Jocko Conlan was on a flight at the beginning of which the stewardess explained what to do in the case of an emergency that required the plane to land in the ocean. None of the bigwigs on the airplane seemed to be listening, so the stewardess got angry, and she said, "I don't care what your rank is or who you are. I'm in charge here and I'm supposed to demonstrate how this life jacket works. If this plane goes down, you're going to need it. If you're too dumb to listen, forget it." Mr. Conlan spoke up: "I'm listening. I can't swim."[241]

• Being an ice dancer is tougher than you think, although it looks effortless on TV. Jayne Torvill and Christopher Dean once performed in an old circus tent in Tasmania. The weather was rough, the tent was leaky, and the audience was forced to use umbrellas while watching the performance. Meanwhile, a half-inch of water collected on the surface of the ice, and Ms. Torvill and Mr. Dean wondered what would happen if the wind blew a live electrical wire down onto the ice.[242]

• When world-class gymnastics coach Bela Karolyi defected from Romania to the United States, he worked like a dog to earn whatever money — usually very little — he could. Often, he and his wife, Marta, ate a pretzel as their food for the entire day. By the way, they did have a dog. The dog ate better than they did, as Mr. Karolyi would feed him table scraps he had gotten from the restaurant where he worked as a cleaner.[243]

• As President, John F. Kennedy appointed his younger brother Robert Kennedy as Attorney General of the United States — a decision for which he was much criticized, in part because Bobby Kennedy was so young and inexperienced. President Kennedy explained his decision in this way: "Bobby wants to practice law, and I thought he ought to get a little experience first."[244]

• In 1997, because President Bill Clinton had injured his foot and couldn't walk to the Orioles' pitcher's mound, Secretary of State Madeleine Albright was given the privilege of throwing the first baseball of Baltimore's season. However, the baseball traveled only 15 feet, and she joked later that she had better not give up her day job.[245]

• Like everyone else, early in his life world-renowned women's gymnastics coach Bela Karolyi had to decide which career to pursue. Once, his mother gave him an appliance to repair. He did his best, but the appliance blew up in his face. Therefore, he decided not to be an engineer, but instead to pursue his interest in gymnastics.[246]

• In the early 20th century, Mr. Fyfe, the Caddie Superintendent at the Royal and Ancient Golf Club at St. Andrews in Scotland, had an interesting way of dealing with disputes between caddies. He simply told them, "Go to the bandstand and fight as long as you can stand, then come back and I'll find you work."[247]

• World-class gymnastics coach Bela Karolyi believes in working his gymnasts hard. When Mary Lou Retton was training with him, she quickly realized that when Mr. Karolyi said, "Just one more," they were really in the middle, not at the end, of the workout.[248]

• Gymnastics coach Steve Nunno can be demanding. When he thinks a gymnast is not working as hard as she should, he kicks her out of practice for awhile. Mr. Nunno has been known to kick as many as 10 of 11 total gymnasts out at one practice.[249]

• Pitcher Lefty Gomez retired from major league baseball, then sought employment elsewhere. A job application form asked for the reason why he had left his previous job, so Lefty wrote, "I couldn't get the side out."[250]

Appendix A: Bibliography

Aller, Susan Bivin. *J.M. Barrie: The Magic Behind Peter Pan*. Minneapolis, MN: Lerner Publications Company, 1994.

Benson, Constance. *Mainly Players: Bensonian Memories*. London: Thornton Butterworth, Ltd., 1926.

Berra, Yogi. *"I Really Didn't Say Everything I Said."* New York: Workman Publishing Company, Inc., 1998.

Berry, Ralph, compiler and editor. *The Methuen Book of Shakespeare Anecdotes*. London: Methuen Drama, 1992.

Boerst, William J. *Isaac Asimov: Writer of the Future*. Greensboro, NC: Morgan Reynolds, Inc., 1999.

Bontemps, Arna. *Famous Negro Athletes*. New York: Dodd, Mead, and Company, 1964.

Brandreth, Gyles. *Great Theatrical Disasters*. New York: St. Martin's Press, 1982.

Brennan, Christine. *Inside Edge: A Revealing Journey into the Secret World of Figure Skating*. New York: Scribner, 1996.

Conlan, Jocko and Robert W. Creamer. *Jocko*. Lincoln, NE: University of Nebraska Press, 1997.

Crawford, John W. *Early Shakespearean Actresses*. New York: Peter Lang Publishing, Inc., 1984.

Dole, Bob. *Great Political Wit*. New York: Doubleday, 1998.

Dole, Bob. *Great Presidential Wit*. New York: Scribner, 2001.

Finlayson, Reggie. *Colin Powell*. Minneapolis, MN: Lerner Publications Company, 1997.

Foster, Leila Merrell. *Benjamin Franklin: Founding Father and Inventor*. Springfield, NJ: Enslow Publications, Inc., 1997.

Garagiola, Joe. *Baseball is a Funny Game*. New York: Bantam Books, 1960.

Garagiola, Joe. *It's Anybody's Ballgame*. New York: Jove Books, 1988.

Gielgud, John. *Distinguished Company*. London: Heinemann, 1972.

Gielgud, John. *Stage Directions*. New York: Random House, 1963.

Gingras, Angele de T. *From Bussing to Bugging: The Best in Congressional Humor*. Washington, D.C.: Acropolis Books, Limited, 1973.

Gorman, Tom, and Jerome Holtzman. *Three and Two!* New York: Charles Scribner's Sons, 1979.

Greenberg, Keith Elliot. *Pro Wrestling: From Carnivals to Cable TV*. Minneapolis, MN: Lerner Publications Company, 2000.

Gregg, Eric, and Marty Appel. *Working the Plate: The Eric Gregg Story*. New York: William Morrow and Company, Inc., 1990.

Guernsey, JoAnn Bren. *Hillary Rodham Clinton: A New Kind of First Lady*. Minneapolis, MN: Lerner Publications Company, 1993.

Guernsey, JoAnn Bren. *Tipper Gore: Voice for the Voiceless*. Minneapolis, MN: Lerner Publications Company, 1994.

Haney, Lynn. *The Lady is a Jock*. New York: Dodd, Mead, and Company, 1973.

Haney, Lynn. *Skaters: Profile of a Pair*. New York: G.P. Putnam's Sons, 1983.

Hanna, Edward; Henry Hicks; and Ted Koppel, compilers. *The Wit and Wisdom of Adlai Stevenson*. New York: Hawthorn Books, Inc., 1965.

Harris, Leon A. *The Fine Art of Political Wit*. New York: Dell Publishing Company, 1964.

Hay, Peter. *Broadway Anecdotes*. New York: Oxford University Press, 1989.

Hayduke, George. *Up Yours! Guide to Advanced Revenge Techniques*. Boulder, CO: Paladin Press, 1982.

Himelstein, Shmuel. *A Touch of Wisdom, A Touch of Wit*. Brooklyn, NY: Mesorah Publications, Limited, 1991.

Himelstein, Shmuel. *Words of Wisdom, Words of Wit*. Brooklyn, NY: Mesorah Publications, Ltd., 1993.

Hintz, Martin. *Farewell, John Barleycorn: Prohibition in the United States*. Minneapolis, MN: Lerner Publications Company, 1996.

Howard, Megan. *Madeleine Albright*. Minneapolis, MN: Lerner Publications Company, 1999.

Huggett, Richard. *Supernatural on Stage: Ghosts and Superstitions of the Theatre*. New York: Taplinger Publishing Company, 1975.

Hull, William H., editor. *Nurse: Heart and Hands*. Edina, MN: William H. Hull Publisher, 1991.

Hyman, Dick. *Potomac Wind and Wisdom: Jokes, Lies, and True Stories By and About America's Politics and Politicians*. Brattleboro, Vermont: The Stephen Greene Press, 1980.

Jerome, Jerome K. *On the Stage — and Off: The Brief Career of a Would-Be Actor*. Wolfeboro Falls, NH: Alan Sutton Publishing, Inc., 1991.

Johnson, Harry "Steamboat." *Standing the Gaff: The Life and Hard Times of a Minor League Umpire*. Introduction to the Bison Book edition by Larry R. Gerlach. Lincoln, NE: University of Nebraska Press, 1994.

Jones, Mrs. George, and Tom Carter. *Nashville Wives*. New York: HarperCollinsPublishers, 1999.

Kane, Jim, and Carmen Germaine Warner, editors. *Touched by a Nurse: Special Moments That Transform Lives*. Philadelphia, PA: Lippincott, 1999.

Kolasky, John, collector and compiler. *Look, Comrade — The People are Laughing* .... Toronto, Ontario: Peter Martin Associates, Limited, 1972.

Kristy, Davida. *Coubertin's Olympics: How the Games Began*. Minneapolis, MN: Lerner Publications Company, 1995.

Lessa, Christina. *Gymnastics Balancing Acts*. New York: Universe Publishing, 1997.

Lessa, Christina. *Women Who Win: Stories of Triumph in Sport and in Life*. New York: Universe Publishing, 1998.

Mackenzie, Richard. *A Wee Nip at the 19th Hole: A History of the St. Andrews Caddie*. Chelsea, MI: Sleeping Bear Press, 1997.

Marcus, Sara. *Girls to the Front: The True Story of the Riot GRRRL Revolution*. New York: Harper Perennial, 2010.

Marinacci, Barbara. *Leading Ladies: A Gallery of Famous Actresses*. New York: Dodd, Mead and Company, 1961.

Marx, Samuel. *Broadway Portraits*. New York: Donald Flamm, Inc., 1929.

May, Robin, compiler. *The Wit of the Theatre*. London: Leslie Frewin, 1969.

McCann, Sean, compiler. *The Wit of Oscar Wilde*. London: Leslie Frewin Publishers, Ltd., 1969.

McCann, Sean, compiler. *The Wit of Brendan Behan*. London: Leslie Frewin Publishers, Ltd., 1968.

Miller, Claudia. *Shannon Miller: My Child, My Hero*. Norman, OK: University of Oklahoma Press, 1999.

Miller, Ernestine Gichner. *The Babe Book*. Kansas City, MO: Andrews McMeel Publishing, 2000.

Miller, John. *Judi Dench: With a Crack in Her Voice*. New York: Welcome Rain Publishers, 2000.

Miller, John. *Ralph Richardson: The Authorized Biography*. London: Sidgwick and Jackson, 1995.

Molen, Sam. *Take 2 and Hit to Right*. Philadelphia, PA: Dorrance and Company, 1959.

Parker, John F. *"If Elected, I Promise ...."* Garden City, NY: Doubleday & Co., Inc., 1960.

Pearson, Hesketh. *Lives of the Wits*. New York: Harper & Row, Publishers, 1962.

Pellowski, Michael J. *Baseball's Funniest People*. New York: Sterling Publishing Co., 1997.

Pike, Robert E. *Granite Laughter and Marble Tears*. Brattleboro, VT: Stephen Daye Press, 1938.

Primack, Ben, adapter and editor. *The Ben Hecht Show: Impolitic Observations from the Freest Thinker of 1950s Television*. Jefferson, NC: McFarland & Company, Inc., Publishers, 1993.

Provenza, Paul, and Dan Dion. *¡Satiristas!: Comedians, Contrarians, Raconteurs & Vulgarians*. New York: HarperCollins Publishers, 2010.

Retton, Mary Lou, and Bela Karolyi. *Mary Lou: Creating an Olympic Champion*. With John Powers. New York: McGraw-Hill Book Company, 1986.

Richards, Dick, compiler. *The Wit of Noël Coward*. London: Leslie Frewin, 1968.

Rigg, Diana, compiler. *No Turn Unstoned: The Worst Ever Theatrical Reviews*. Los Angeles, CA: Silman-James Press, 1982.

Rogers, Fred. *The World According to Mister Rogers*. New York: Hyperion, 2003.

Rossi, Alfred. *Astonish Us in the Morning: Tyrone Guthrie Remembered*. London: Hutchinson & Co., Publishers, 1977.

Rosten, Leo. *People I Have Loved, Known or Admired*. New York: McGraw-Hill Book Company, 1970.

Ruksenas, Algis. *Is That You Laughing Comrade? The World's Best Russian (Underground) Jokes*. Secaucus, NJ: Citadel Press, 1986.

Russell, Fred. *I'll Try Anything Twice*. Nashville, TN: The McQuiddy Press, 1945.

Russell, Mark, editor. *Out of Character*. New York: Bantam Books, 1997.

Savage, Jeff. *Tiger Woods: King of the Course*. Minneapolis, MN: Lerner Publications Company, 1998.

Schraff, Anne. *Ralph Bunche: Winner of the Nobel Peace Prize*. Berkeley Heights, NJ: Enslow Publications, Inc., 1999.

Schulman, Arlene. *Muhammad Ali: Champion*. Minneapolis, MN: Lerner Publications Company, 1996.

Skipper, John C. *Umpires: Classic Baseball Stories from the Men Who Made the Calls*. Jefferson, NC, and London: McFarland and Company, Inc., Publishers, 1997.

Smith, Beverley. *Figure Skating: A Celebration*. Toronto, Ontario, Canada: McClelland & Stewart, Inc., 1994.

Smith, Ira L. and H. Allen Smith. *Low and Inside*. Garden City, NY: Doubleday and Company, Inc., 1949.

Smith, Ira L., and H. Allen Smith. *Three Men on Third*. New York: Doubleday & Co., Inc., 1951.

Snead, Sam. *The Game I Love: Wisdom, Insight, and Instruction from Golf's Greatest Player*. With Fran Pirozzolo. New York: Ballantine Books, 1997.

Sobol, Donald J. *Encyclopedia Brown's Book of Wacky Sports*. New York: William Morrow and Company, 1984.

Spalding, Henry D. *Jewish Laffs*. Middle Village, NY: Jonathan David Publishers, Inc., 1982.

Stephens, Autumn. *Wild Women in the White House*. Berkeley, CA: Conari Press, 1997.

Strug, Kerri. *Landing on My Feet: A Diary of Dreams*. With John P. Lopez. Kansas City, MO: Andrews McMeel Publishing, 1997.

Sullivan, George. *Any Number Can Play*. New York: Thomas Y. Crowell, 1990.

Swisher, Clarice. *Pablo Picasso*. San Diego, CA: Lucent Books, 1995.

Tanner, Stephen. *Opera Antics and Anecdotes*. Toronto, Canada: Sound and Vision, 1999.

Telushkin, Rabbi Joseph. *Jewish Humor: What the Best Jewish Jokes Say About the Jews*. New York: William Morrow and Company, 1992.

Telushkin, Rabbi Joseph. *Jewish Wisdom: Ethical, Spiritual, and Historical Lessons from the Great Works and Thinkers*. New York: William Morrow and Company, Inc., 1994.

Thomas, Kurt, and Kent Hannon. *Kurt Thomas on Gymnastics*. New York: Simon and Schuster, 1980.

Thompson, Joe. *Growing Up with "Shoeless Joe."* Greenville, SC: Burgess International, 1997.

Torvill, Jayne, and Christopher Dean. *Torvill and Dean: The Autobiography of Ice Dancing's Greatest Stars*. With John Man. Secaucus, NJ: Carol Publishing Group, 1996.

Tsai, Chih-Chung. *Zen Speaks: Shouts of Nothingness*. New York: Anchor Books, 1994.

Udall, Morris K. *Too Funny to be President*. With Bob Neuman and Randy Udall. New York: Henry Holt and Company, 1988.

Uecker, Bob, and Mickey Herskowitz. *Catcher in the Wry*. New York: G.P. Putnam's Sons, 1982.

Van Dyke, Dick. *Faith, Hope and Hilarity*. Edited by Ray Parker. Garden City, NY: Doubleday and Company, Inc, 1970.

Verstraete, Larry. *At the Edge: Daring Acts in Desperate Times*. New York: Scholastic Inc. 2009.

Wade, Don. *"And Then Arnie Told Chi Chi ...."* Chicago, IL: Contemporary Books, 1993.

Wagenknecht, Edward. *Merely Players*. Norman, OK: University of Oklahoma Press, 1966.

Wagenknecht, Edward. *Seven Daughters of the Theater*. Norman, OK: University of Oklahoma Press, 1964.

Waldron, Ann. *Claude Monet*. New York: Harry N. Abrams, Inc., 1991.

Ward, Hiley H., editor. *Ecumania: The Humor That Happens When Catholics, Jews, and Protestants Come Together*. New York: Association Press, 1968.

Wiesel, Elie. *Souls on Fire: Portraits and Legends of Hasidic Masters*. Translated from the French by Marion Wiesel. New York: Random House, 1972.

Woollcott, Alexander. *Enchanted Aisles*. New York: G.P. Putnam's Sons, 1924.

Woollcott, Alexander. *Shouts and Murmurs: Echoes of a Thousand and One Nights*. New York: The Century Co., 1922.

Wordsworth, R. D., compiler. *"Abe" Lincoln's Anecdotes and Stories*. Boston, MA: The Mutual Book Company, 1908.

Wright, David K. *Arthur Ashe: Breaking the Color Barrier in Tennis*. Springfield, NJ: Enslow Publications, Inc., 1996.

Whistler, James Abbott McNeill. *The Gentle Art of Making Enemies*. New York: Dover Publications, Inc., 1967.

Yungshans, Penelope. *Prize Winners: Ten Writers for Young People*. Greensboro, NC: Morgan Reynolds, Inc., 1995.

Zall, P.M. *George Washington Laughing: Humorous Anecdotes by and about our first President from Original Sources*. Hamden, CN: Archon Books, 1989.

Zall, Paul M. *The Wit and Wisdom of the Founding Fathers*. Hopewell, New Jersey: The Ecco Press, 1996.

Appendix B: About the Author

It was a dark and stormy night. Suddenly a cry rang out, and on a hot summer night in 1954, Josephine, wife of Carl Bruce, gave birth to a boy — me. Unfortunately, this young married couple allowed Reuben Saturday, Josephine's brother, to name their first-born. Reuben, aka "The Joker," decided that Bruce was a nice name, so he decided to name me Bruce Bruce. I have gone by my middle name — David — ever since.

Being named Bruce David Bruce hasn't been all bad. Bank tellers remember me very quickly, so I don't often have to show an ID. It can be fun in charades, also. When I was a counselor as a teenager at Camp Echoing Hills in Warsaw, Ohio, a fellow counselor gave the signs for "sounds like" and "two words," then she pointed to a bruise on her leg twice. Bruise Bruise? Oh yeah, Bruce Bruce is the answer!

Uncle Reuben, by the way, gave me a haircut when I was in kindergarten. He cut my hair short and shaved a small bald spot on the back of my head. My mother wouldn't let me go to school until the bald spot grew out again.

Of all my brothers and sisters (six in all), I am the only transplant to Athens, Ohio. I was born in Newark, Ohio, and have lived all around Southeastern Ohio. However, I moved to Athens to go to Ohio University and have never left.

At Ohio U, I never could make up my mind whether to major in English or Philosophy, so I got a bachelor's degree with a double major in both areas, then I added a Master of Arts degree in English and a Master of Arts degree in Philosophy. Yes, I have my MAMA degree.

Currently, and for a long time to come (I eat fruits and veggies), I am spending my retirement writing books such as *Nadia Comaneci: Perfect 10*, *The Funniest People in Comedy*, *Homer's* Iliad: *A Retelling in Prose*, and *William Shakespeare's* Hamlet: *A Retelling in Prose*.

If all goes well, I will publish one or two books a year for the rest of my life. (On the other hand, a good way to make God laugh is to tell Her your plans.)

By the way, my sister Brenda Kennedy writes romances such as *A New Beginning* and *Shattered Dreams*.

Appendix C: Some Books by David Bruce

Anecdote Collections

250 Anecdotes About Opera
250 Anecdotes About Religion
250 Anecdotes About Religion: Volume 2
250 Music Anecdotes
Be a Work of Art: 250 Anecdotes and Stories
Boredom is Anti-Life: 250 Anecdotes and Stories
The Coolest People in Art: 250 Anecdotes
The Coolest People in the Arts: 250 Anecdotes
The Coolest People in Books: 250 Anecdotes
The Coolest People in Comedy: 250 Anecdotes
Create, Then Take a Break: 250 Anecdotes
Don't Fear the Reaper: 250 Anecdotes
The Funniest People in Art: 250 Anecdotes
The Funniest People in Books: 250 Anecdotes
The Funniest People in Books, Volume 2: 250 Anecdotes
The Funniest People in Books, Volume 3: 250 Anecdotes
The Funniest People in Comedy: 250 Anecdotes
The Funniest People in Dance: 250 Anecdotes
The Funniest People in Families: 250 Anecdotes
The Funniest People in Families, Volume 2: 250 Anecdotes
The Funniest People in Families, Volume 3: 250 Anecdotes
The Funniest People in Families, Volume 4: 250 Anecdotes
The Funniest People in Families, Volume 5: 250 Anecdotes
The Funniest People in Families, Volume 6: 250 Anecdotes
The Funniest People in Movies: 250 Anecdotes
The Funniest People in Music: 250 Anecdotes
The Funniest People in Music, Volume 2: 250 Anecdotes
The Funniest People in Music, Volume 3: 250 Anecdotes
The Funniest People in Neighborhoods: 250 Anecdotes
The Funniest People in Relationships: 250 Anecdotes
The Funniest People in Sports: 250 Anecdotes
The Funniest People in Sports, Volume 2: 250 Anecdotes
The Funniest People in Television and Radio: 250 Anecdotes

The Funniest People in Theater: 250 Anecdotes
The Funniest People Who Live Life: 250 Anecdotes
The Funniest People Who Live Life, Volume 2: 250 Anecdotes
The Kindest People Who Do Good Deeds, Volume 1: 250 Anecdotes
The Kindest People Who Do Good Deeds, Volume 2: 250 Anecdotes
Maximum Cool: 250 Anecdotes
The Most Interesting People in Movies: 250 Anecdotes
The Most Interesting People in Politics and History: 250 Anecdotes
The Most Interesting People in Politics and History, Volume 2: 250 Anecdotes
The Most Interesting People in Politics and History, Volume 3: 250 Anecdotes
The Most Interesting People in Religion: 250 Anecdotes
The Most Interesting People in Sports: 250 Anecdotes
The Most Interesting People Who Live Life: 250 Anecdotes
The Most Interesting People Who Live Life, Volume 2: 250 Anecdotes
Reality is Fabulous: 250 Anecdotes and Stories
Resist Psychic Death: 250 Anecdotes
Seize the Day: 250 Anecdotes and Stories

[1] Source: Edward Wagenknecht, *Merely Players*, p. 4.

[2] Source: Ralph Berry, compiler and editor, *The Methuen Book of Shakespeare Anecdotes*, p. 81.

[3] Source: John W. Crawford, *Early Shakespearean Actresses*, pp. 21-22.

[4] Source: John Miller, *Judi Dench: With a Crack in Her Voice*, p. 235.

[5] Source: Diana Rigg, compiler, *No Turn Unstoned*, p. 38.

[6] Source: Barbara Marinacci, *Leading Ladies: A Gallery of Famous Actresses*, p. 192.

[7] Source: Dick Richards, compiler, *The Wit of Noël Coward*, p. 15.

[8] Source: "'Occupy the Tundra': One woman's lonely vigil in bush Alaska." *Los Angeles Times* Blogs. 15 October 2011 <http://latimesblogs.latimes.com/nationnow/2011/10/bethel-occupy-the-tundra-facebook.html>.

[9] Source: "4TH AMENDMENT UNDERCLOTHES: For When Unwarranted Searches Go Too Far." <http://cargocollective.com/4thamendment>. <http://cargocollective.com/4thamendment#806188/About   >. <http://cargocollective.com/4thamendment#799841/Perverts-Printed-Kid-s-Underclothes>. Accessed 13 September 2011. For more information, contact 4TH AMENDMENT WEAR, PO BOX 6122, BOULDER CO 80306 or go to <http://cargocollective.com/4thamendment#799609/Home>.

[10] Source: Patrick Barkham, "Angry US taxpayers stamp on companies paying no corporate tax." *Guardian* (UK). 11 September 2011 <http://www.guardian.co.uk/world/2011/sep/11/american-taxpayers-defacing-dollar-bills>. Also: DAVID KOCIENIEWSKI, "G.E.'s Strategies Let It Avoid Taxes Altogether." *New York Times*. 24 MARCH 2011 <http://tinyurl.com/6ykmq3e>.

[11] Source: Donald J. Sobol, *Encyclopedia Brown's Book of Wacky Sports*, pp. 107-108.

[12] Source: Alexander Woollcott, *Enchanted Aisles*, p. 230.

[13] Source: Shmuel Himelstein, *Words of Wisdom, Words of Wit*, p. 29.

[14] Source: Alfred Rossi, *Astonish Us in the Morning*, pp. 16, 133, 155.

[15] Source: Stephen Tanner, *Opera Antics and Anecdotes*, p. 88.

[16] Source: P. M. Zall, *George Washington Laughing*, pp. 11-12.

[17] Source: Sean McCann, compiler, *The Wit of Brendan Behan*, pp. 57-58, 139.

[18] Source: Hesketh Pearson, *Lives of the Wits*, pp. 118-119.

[19] Source: Scott Stump, "Firefighter revives dog, mouth to snout. Pooch carried unconscious out of a burning home is saved by quick-thinking rescue." TODAY.com. 21 October 2011 <http://today.msnbc.msn.com/id/44987964/ns/today-good_news/#.TqQIZ2B2kVk>.

[20] Source: Alexander Woollcott, *Shouts and Murmurs*, pp. 234-235.

[21] Source: Christina Lessa, *Women Who Win*, p. 63.

[22] Source: John Gielgud, *Distinguished Company*, p. 18.

[23] Source: Robert E. Pike, *Granite Laughter and Marble Tears*, p. 31.

[24] Source: Larry Verstraete, *At the Edge: Daring Acts in Desperate Time*, p. 131. Also: Mark Landler, "A NATION CHALLENGED: CULTURE; An Afghan Artist Erases Layers of Taliban Repression." New York Times. 13 January 2001 <http://www.nytimes.com/2002/01/13/world/a-nation-challenged-culture-an-afghan-artist-erases-layers-of-taliban-repression.html?n=Top%2fReference%2fTimes%20Topics%2fSubjects%2fT%2fTerrori

[25] Source: Clarice Swisher, *Pablo Picasso*, pp. 64, 71.

[26] Source: Ann Waldron, *Claude Monet*, pp. 46-47.

[27] Source: Alfred Werner, "Introduction" to James Abbott McNeill Whistler's *The Gentle Art of Making Enemies*, p. ix.

[28] Source: Jerome K. Jerome, *On the Stage — and Off*, p. 49.

[29] Source: Robin May, compiler, *The Wit of the Theatre*, p. 57.

[30] Source: Ira L. Smith and H. Allen Smith, *Low and Inside*, pp. 98-99.

[31] Source: Joe Garagiola, *Baseball is a Funny Game*, p. 59.

[32] Source: Eric Gregg and Marty Appel, *Working the Plate*, p. 150.

[33] Source: Alfred Werner, "Introduction" to James Abbott McNeill Whistler's *The Gentle Art of Making Enemies*, pp. xvii-xix.

[34] Source: William J. Boerst, *Isaac Asimov: Writer of the Future*, pp. 88, 90.

[35] Source: Rabbi Joseph Telushkin, *Jewish Wisdom*, p. 20.

[36] Source: Yogi Berra, *"I Really Didn't Say Everything I Said,"* p. 111.

[37] Source: Penelope Yungshans, *Prize Winners: Ten Writers for Young People*, pp. 12-13, 20.

[38] Source: Roger Ebert, "Mary we crown thee with blossoms today!" Roger Ebert's Journal. 4 August 2010 <http://blogs.suntimes.com/ebert/2010/08/o_mary_we_crown_thee_with_blos.html>.

[39] Source: Reggie Finlayson, *Colin Powell: People's Hero*, pp. 17-19.

[40] Source: William J. Boerst, *Isaac Asimov: Writer of the Future*, pp. 10-11, 14.

[41] Source: JoAnn Bren Guernsey, *Hillary Rodham Clinton: A New Kind of First Lady*, pp. 23-24.

[42] Source: Christina Lessa, *Gymnastics Balancing Acts*, p. 4.

[43] Source: Arlene Schulman, *Muhammad Ali: Champion*, p. 15.

[44] Source: Bob Dole, *Great Political Wit*, p. 74.

[45] Source: Dick Van Dyke, *Faith, Hope, and Hilarity*, pp. 95-6.

[46] Source: Mark Russell, editor, *Out of Character*, p. 93.

[47] Source: Bob Dole, *Great Political Wit*, pp. 18-19.

[48] Source: Dick Van Dyke, *Faith, Hope, and Hilarity*, pp. 11, 35.

[49] Source: Dick Hymen, *Potomac Wind and Wisdom*, p. 13.

[50] Source: Arna Bontemps, *Famous Negro Athletes*, pp. 34-35.

[51] Source: Christine Brennan, *Inside Edge*, p. 15.

[52] Source: Don Wade, *"And Then Arnie Told Chi Chi...,"* p. 78.

[53] Source: Lynn Haney, *The Lady is a Jock*, p. 16.

[54] Source: Dick Richards, compiler, *The Wit of Noël Coward*, p. 94.

[55] Source: David K. Wright, *Arthur Ashe: Breaking the Color Barrier in Tennis*, p. 111.

[56] Source: Sean McCann, compiler, *The Wit of Oscar Wilde*, pp. 14, 56.

[57] Source: Diana Rigg, compiler, *No Turn Unstoned*, p. 113.

[58] Source: Edward Wagenknecht, *Merely Players*, p. 4.

[59] Source: Jim Kane and Carmen Germaine Warner, editors, *Touched by a Nurse: Special Moments That Transform Lives*, p. 100.

[60] Source: Rabbi Joseph Telushkin, *Jewish Wisdom*, pp. 218-219.

[61] Source: Jim Kane and Carmen Germaine Warner, editors, *Touched by a Nurse: Special Moments That Transform Lives*, p. 47

[62] Source: Paul Provenza and Dan Dion, *¡Satiristas!: Comedians, Contrarians, Raconteurs & Vulgarians*, p. 307.

[63] Source: Robert E. Pike, *Granite Laughter and Marble Tears*, p. 54.

[64] Source: Ben Primack, adapter and editor, *The Ben Hecht Show*, p. 46.

[65] Source: Sara Marcus, *Girls to the Front: The True Story of the Riot GRRRL Revolution*, pp. 37, 60-70.

[66] Source: John Kolasky, collector and compiler, *Look, Comrade — The People are Laughing...*, p. 19.

[67] Source: Paul M. Zall, *The Wit and Wisdom of the Founding Fathers*, pp. 34-35.

[68] Source: Elie Wiesel, *Souls on Fire*, pp. 117-118.

[69] Source: Connie Schultz, "Share Your Stories, Teachers." Creators Syndicate. 2 September 2011 <http://www.creators.com/liberal/connie-schultz/share-your-stories-teachers.html>.

[70] Source: Megan Howard, *Madeleine Albright*, p. 37.

[71] Source: Chih Chung Tsai, *Zen Speaks*, p. 32.

[72] Source: JoAnn Bren Guernsey, *Hillary Rodham Clinton: A New Kind of First Lady*, p. 7.

[73] Source: Kurt Thomas and Kent Hannon, *Kurt Thomas on Gymnastics*, p. 64.

[74] Source: Beverley Smith, *Figure Skating: A Celebration*, p. 236.

[75] Source: Kerri Strug, *Landing on My Feet*, p. 34.

[76] Source: Barbara Marinacci, *Leading Ladies: A Gallery of Famous Actresses*, pp. 226-228.

[77] Source: Lynn Haney, *Skaters: Profile of a Pair*, p. 40.

[78] Source: Richard Huggett, *Supernatural on Stage*, p. 211.

[79] Source: Anthony Herrera, "This is What Happens When Your Dad's A Graphic Designer: Ewoks!" Anthony Herrera Designs. 20 September 2011 <http://anthonyherreradesigns.com/ index.php?option=com_content&view=article&id=53:this-is-what-happens-when-your-dads-a-graphic-designer-ewoks&catid=34:anthonydesign-blog>.

[80] Source: Clarice Swisher, *Pablo Picasso*, pp. 16, 18.

[81] Source: Jeff Savage, *Tiger Woods: King of the Course*, p. 17.

[82] Source: Penelope Yungshans, *Prize Winners: Ten Writers for Young People*, p. 82.

[83] Source: Davida Kristy, *Coubertin's Olympics*, p. 80.

[84] Source: Christina Lessa, *Women Who Win*, p. 59.

[85] Source: Constance Benson, *Mainly Players*, p. 103.

[86] Source: Shmuel Himelstein, *Words of Wisdom, Words of Wit*, p. 69.

[87] Source: Sam Molen, *Take 2 and Hit to Right*, p. 104.

[88] Source: Jeff Savage, *Tiger Woods: King of the Course*, p, 59.

[89] Source: Richard Mackenzie, *A Wee Nip at the 19th Hole*, pp. 38-39.

[90] Source: Sam Snead, *The Game I Love*, pp. 97-98.

[91] Source: Sam Molen, *Take 2 and Hit to Right*, p. 119.

[92] Source: Jeff Savage, *Julie Foudy: Soccer Superstar*, p. 53.

[93] Source: Moral12, "Setting Up an Apartment for a Girl in Need." Helpothers.org. 6 September 2011 <http://www.helpothers.org/ story.php?sid=27617>.

[94] Source: Natasha Ryan: "Girl reunited with 'Daddy Bear' lost on busy interstate." KING5. 14 October 2011 <http://www.msnbc.msn.com/id/44903980/ ns/local_news-seattle_wa/#.TpmASGB2kVk>.

[95] Source: John Adams, "Flowers for Mom." Stories of Kindness. Kindness USA. <http://www.kindnessusa.org/storiesofkindness.htm>. Accessed 27 September 2011.

[96] Source: Jaybird, "Customer's Gift to an Employee." HelpOthers.org. 26 July 2011 <http://www.helpothers.org/story.php?sid=26925>.

[97] Source: Don Wade, *"And Then Arnie Told Chi Chi...,"* p. 138.

[98] Source: Harry "Steamboat" Johnson, *Standing the Gaff*, pp. xxviii, 91.

[99] Source: Laura Caroe, "My son saved my life." *Evening Chronicle* (Newcastle, England). 28 June 2007 <http://www.chroniclelive.co.uk/north-east-news/ evening-chronicle-news/ tm_headline=my-son-saved-my-life&method=full&objectid=19372380&siteid=50081

[100] Source: Tom Hallman Jr., "Woman trapped in Milwaukie fire trusted stranger to save a child; two other children died." *The Oregonian*. 12 February 2011

<http://www.oregonlive.com/milwaukie/index.ssf/2011/02/ woman_trapped_in_milwaukie_fire_trusted_stranger_with_her_child.html>.

[101] Source: Angelica Martinez, "12-year old boy takes charge at city airport: Credited with saving pilot from serious accident." *The San Bernardino Sun* (CA). 5 November 2002 <http://archives.californiaaviation.org/ganews/msg10265.html>. Also: Larry Verstraete, *At the Edge: Daring Acts in Desperate Time*, p. 84. Also: Richard Jerome, Susan Schindehette, "Their Finest Hour." *People* (Vol. 58, No. 24). 9 December 2002 <http://www.people.com/people/archive/article/ 0,,20138700,00.html>.

[102] Source: "Woman plucked from subway tracks meets her angels." Good News Blog. 6 November 2005 <http://www.goodnewsblog.com/2005/11/06/ woman-plucked-from-subway-tracks-meets-her-angels>. This article may have originally appeared in the *Toronto Star*.

[103] Source: Ana Facio Contreras, "Oakland boy becomes a hero to his family." Contra Costa Times (Walnut Creek, CA). 27 August 2001 <http://www.contracostatimes.com/mld/cctimes/news/6628576.htm>. Posted at Real Life Little Heroes <http://www.chinastrategies.com/ lithero.htm#Oakland%20boy%20becomes%20a%20hero%20to%20his%20family>.

[104] Source: Richard Jerome, Susan Schindehette, "Their Finest Hour." *People* (Vol. 58, No. 24). 9 December 2002 <http://www.people.com/people/archive/ article/0,,20138700,00.html>.

[105] Source: Karen Bale, "MY HERO; Brave Connor plunges 20feet into river to save drowning sister Gemma." Daily Record (Glasgow, Scotland). 29 June 2007 <http://www.thefreelibrary.com/ MY+HERO%3B+Brave+Connor+plunges+20feet+into+river+to+save+drowning...-a016…

[106] Source: "9 year old boy honored as hero." KRIS-TV. Date not given. <http://www.kristv.com/Global/story.asp?S=1458294>. Posted at Real Life Little Heroes <http://www.chinastrategies.com/ lithero.htm#9%20year%20old%20boy%20honored%20as%20hero>. Accessed 13 September 2011.

[107] Source: Richard Jerome and Susan Schindehette, "Their Finest Hour." *People* (Vol. 58, No. 24). 9 December 2002 <http://www.people.com/people/ archive/article/0,,20138700,00.html>.

[108] Source: "I married my hero." Good News Blog. 13 February 2005 <http://www.goodnewsblog.com/2005/02/13/i-married-my-hero>.

[109] Source: Mrs. George Jones and Tom Carter, *Nashville Wives*, pp. 115-116.

[110] Source: JoAnn Bren Guernsey, *Tipper Gore: Voice for the Voiceless*, pp. 11, 14-15, 23, 58.

[111] Source: Rabbi Joseph Telushkin, *Jewish Wisdom*, p. 365.

[112] Source: John W. Crawford, *Early Shakespearean Actresses*, p. 155.

[113] Source: Mrs. George Jones and Tom Carter, *Nashville Wives*, pp. 3-4.

[114] Source: Fred Rogers, *The World According to Mister Rogers*, p. 4

[115] Source: Tom Mullen, "Ice show is real cool; CARTOON HEROES PUT ON A SPECTACULAR DISPLAY: FOR THEIR YOUNG FANS ON TYNESIDE." *Evening Chronicle* (Newcastle, England). 6 October 2010 <http://findarticles.com/p/articles/mi_6783/is_2010_Oct_6/ ai_n55464676/?tag=content;col1>.

[116] Source: Jocko Conlan and Robert W. Creamer, *Jocko*, p. 90.

[117] Source: Martin Hintz, *Farewell, John Barleycorn: Prohibition in the United States*, pp. 34, 39.

[118] Source: Stephen Tanner, *Opera Antics and Anecdotes*, p. 92.

[119] Source: John C. Skipper, *Umpires*, p. 94.

[120] Source: Leila Merrell Foster, *Benjamin Franklin: Founding Father and Inventor*, pp. 13, 15.

[121] Source: Morris K. Udall, *Too Funny to be President*, p. 18.

[122] Source: Leo Rosten, *People I Have Loved, Known or Admired*, p. 88.

[123] Source: Eve Ensler, *The Vagina Monologues*, p. 165. Of course, Ms. Ensler does not use the asterisks. The writer of the book you are reading now is a w*mp.

[124] Source: Yogi Berra, *"I Really Didn't Say Everything I Said,"* p. 57.

[125] Source: George Hayduke, *Up Yours! Guide to Advanced Revenge Techniques*, p. 67.

[126] Source: Paul M. Zall, *The Wit and Wisdom of the Founding Fathers*, pp. 99, 118.

[127] Source: Samuel Marx, *Broadway Portraits*, p. 18.

[128] Source: Joe Thompson, *Growing Up with "Shoeless Joe,"* pp. 86-87.

[129] Source: Tom Gorman and Jerome Holtzman, *Three and Two!*, p. 59.

[130] Source: Jayne Torvill and Christopher Dean, *Torvill and Dean*, p. 123.

[131] Source: Joe Garagiola, *It's Anybody's Ballgame*, p. 238.

[132] Source: Edward Wagenknecht, *Seven Daughters of the Theater*, p. 130.

[133] Source: Samuel Marx, *Broadway Portraits*, pp. 12-13.

[134] Source: William H. Hull, editor, *Nurse: Heart and Hands*, pp. 189-190.

[135] Source: Alexander Woollcott, *Shouts and Murmurs*, pp. 3-4.

[136] Source: Fred Russell, *I'll Try Anything Twice*, p. 99.

[137] Source: Richard Huggett, *Supernatural on Stage*, p. 193.

[138] Source: Gyles Brandreth, *Great Theatrical Disasters*, p. xi.

[139] Source: John Miller, *Ralph Richardson*, p. 79.

[140] Source: Joe Thompson, *Growing Up with "Shoeless Joe,"* pp. 153-154, 252-253.

[141] Source: "Beggar 'making more money by feigning invisibility.'" *Metro* (UK). 23 September 2011 <http://www.metro.co.uk/weird/876429-beggar-making-more-money-by-feigning-invisibility#ixzz1Z3Tf4xoj>.

[142] Source: Sam Snead, *The Game I Love*, pp. 106, 146-147, 208.

[143] Source: Lynn Haney, *The Lady is a Jock*, pp. 147-148.

[144] Source: Bob Dole, *Great Presidential Wit*, p. 34.

[145] Source: Leo Rosten, *People I Have Loved, Known or Admired*, p. 68.

[146] Source: Michael Inbar, "Mom's hug revives baby that was pronounced dead." TODAY.com. 3 September 2011 <http://today.msnbc.msn.com/id/38988444/ns/today-parenting/t/moms-hug-revives-baby-was-pronounced-dead/#.Trvodc014no>.

[147] Source: JoAnn Bren Guernsey, *Tipper Gore: Voice for the Voiceless*, pp. 13, 21-22, 24, 26-27.

[148] Source: Robin May, compiler, *The Wit of the Theatre*, p. 124.

[149] Source: Chaya Babu. "Name changers: 285 Indian girls no longer 'unwanted': District Hopes Renaming Ceremony will Give Girls New Dignity, Fight Discrimination." Associated Press. 22 October 2011 <http://www.msnbc.msn.com/id/44998378/ns/world_news-wonderful_world/#.TqWyKmA14np>.

[150] Source: Arlene Schulman, *Muhammad Ali: Champion*, pp. 10-11, 50.

[151] Source: John F. Parker, *"If Elected, I Promise ...."*, p. 112.

[152] Source: Christine Brennan, *Inside Edge*, p. 15.

[153] Source: Claudia Miller, *Shannon Miller: My Child, My Hero*, p. 112.

[154] Source: William H. Hull, editor, *Nurse: Heart and Hands*, pp. 41-43.

[155] Source: John Kolasky, collector and compiler, *Look, Comrade — The People are Laughing ...*, p. 63.

[156] Source: Angele de T. Gingras, *From Bussing to Bugging*, pp. 100-101.

[157] Source: Leon A. Harris, *The Fine Art of Political Wit*, p. 86.

[158] Source: Edward Hanna, Henry Hicks, and Ted Koppel, compilers, *The Wit and Wisdom of Adlai Stevenson*, pp. 66, 68.

[159] Source: Henry D. Spalding, *Jewish Laffs*, p. 94.

[160] Source: Autumn Stephens, *Wild Women in the White House*, p. 1`58.

[161] Source: Morris K. Udall, *Too Funny to be President*, p. 10.

[162] Source: John F. Parker, *"If Elected, I Promise ...."*, p. 25.

[163] Source: Autumn Stephens, *Wild Women in the White House*, p. 122.

[164] Source: John Miller, *Judi Dench: With a Crack in Her Voice*, pp. 2-3, 280.

[165] Source: Michael J. Pellowski, *Baseball's Funniest People*, pp. 57-59.

[166] Source: Fred Russell, *I'll Try Anything Twice*, p. 8.

[167] Source: Constance Benson, *Mainly Players*, p. 92.

[168] Source: Bob Uecker and Mickey Herskowitz, *Catcher in the Wry*, pp. 217-218.

[169] Source: Elie Wiesel, *Souls on Fire*, p. 73.

[170] Source: Shmuel Himelstein, *A Touch of Wisdom, A Touch of Wit*, p. 265.

[171] Source: Bob Uecker and Mickey Herskowitz, *Catcher in the Wry*, p. 212.

[172] Source: Davida Kristy, *Coubertin's Olympics*, p. 113.

[173] Source: Anne Schraff, *Ralph Bunche: Winner of the Nobel Peace Prize*, p. 20.

[174] Source: Peter Hay, *Broadway Anecdotes*, p. 37.

[175] Source: George Hayduke, *Up Yours! Guide to Advanced Revenge Techniques*, pp. 41-42.

[176] Source: Roger Ebert, "'I got in!' and other tales, and the great beauties of the festival." 23 May 2009 <http://blogs.suntimes.com/ebert/2009/05/cannes_9_i_got_in_and_other_st.html>.

[177] Source: Ben Primack, adapter and editor, *The Ben Hecht Show*, pp. 124-125.

[178] Source: Henry Chu, "In Britain, some schools banning skirts." *Los Angeles Times*. 10 September 2011 <http://www.latimes.com/news/nationworld/world/la-fg-britain-school-uniforms-20110911,0,4597904.story>.

[179] Source: Ann Waldron, *Claude Monet*, p. 77.

[180] Source: Ira L. Smith and H. Allen Smith, *Low and Inside*, pp. 121-122.

[181] Source: Leila Merrell Foster, *Benjamin Franklin: Founding Father and Inventor*, p. 17.

[182] Source: Peter Hay, *Broadway Anecdotes*, p. 266.

[183] Source: Algis Ruksenas, *Is That You Laughing Comrade?*, p. 145.

[184] Source: Martin Hintz, *Farewell, John Barleycorn: Prohibition in the United States*, p. 43.

[185] Source: Ira L. Smith and H. Allen Smith, *Three Men on Third*, pp. 194-195.

[186] Source: Sara Marcus, *Girls to the Front: The True Story of the Riot GRRRL Revolution*, pp. 279-280.

[187] Source: Fred Rogers, *The World According to Mister Rogers*, p. 110.

[188] Source: George Sullivan, *Any Number Can Play*, p. 45.

[189] Source: Edward Wagenknecht, *Seven Daughters of the Theater*, p. 78.

[190] Source: Leon A. Harris, *The Fine Art of Political Wit*, p. 265.

[191] Source: R. D. Wordsworth, compiler, *"Abe" Lincoln's Anecdotes and Stories*, p. 17.

[192] Source: Joe Garagiola, *Baseball is a Funny Game*, p. 84.

[193] Source: Donald J. Sobol, *Encyclopedia Brown's Book of Wacky Sports*, p. 110.

[194] Source: Eric Gregg and Marty Appel, *Working the Plate*, p. 162.

[195] Source: Jerome K. Jerome, *On the Stage — and Off*, pp. 140-141.

[196] Source: Ernestine Gichner Miller, *The Babe Book*, p. 156.

[197] Source: Anne Schraff, *Ralph Bunche: Winner of the Nobel Peace Prize*, p. 77.

[198] Source: Shmuel Himelstein, *A Touch of Wisdom, A Touch of Wit*, p. 204.

[199] Source: Rabbi Joseph Telushkin, *Jewish Humor*, p. 143.

[200] Source: Hiley H. Ward, editor, *Ecumania*, p. 69.

[201] Source: Angele de T. Gingras, *From Bussing to Bugging*, p. 97.

[202] Source: Edward Hanna, Henry Hicks, and Ted Koppel, compilers, *The Wit and Wisdom of Adlai Stevenson*, p. 90.

[203] Source: Josh Fjelstad, "Best Of Hurricane Irene Store Signs." Buzzfeed. <http://www.buzzfeed.com/fjelstud/hurricane-irene-store-signs>. Accessed on 29 August 2011.

[204] Source: Henry D. Spalding, *Jewish Laffs*, p. 36.

[205] Source: Paul Provenza and Dan Dion, *¡Satiristas!: Comedians, Contrarians, Raconteurs & Vulgarians*, p. 97.

[206] Source: Jeff Savage, *Julie Foudy: Soccer Superstar*, p. 11.

[207] Source: Tom Danehy, "Tom is definitely not a fan of Thursday-night college football." *Tucson Weekly* (Arizona). 27 October 2011 <http://www.tucsonweekly.com/tucson/danehy/Content?oid=3171615>.

[208] Source: George Sullivan, *Any Number Can Play*, pp. 16-17.

[209] Source: Kurt Thomas and Kent Hannon, *Kurt Thomas on Gymnastics*, p. 43.

[210] Source: Lynn Haney, *Skaters: Profile of a Pair*, p. 30.

[211] Source: Beverley Smith, *Figure Skating: A Celebration*, p. 44.

[212] Source: Susan Bivin Aller, *J.M. Barrie: The Magic Behind Peter Pan*, pp. 7, 80, 89.

[213] Source: Ralph Berry, compiler and editor, *The Methuen Book of Shakespeare Anecdotes*, pp. 135-136.

[214] Source: Eve Ensler, *The Vagina Monologues*, pp. xxviii, 150.

[215] Source: Hesketh Pearson, *Lives of the Wits*, pp. 200, 208.

[216] Source: Gyles Brandreth, *Great Theatrical Disasters*, pp. 86-87.

[217] Source: John Gielgud, *Stage Directions*, p. 54.

[218] Source: Alfred Rossi, *Astonish Us in the Morning*, p. 33.

[219] Source: John Miller, *Ralph Richardson*, p. 290.

[220] Source: Tonya Fennell, "Brother gives gift of life to sister with leukemia after bone marrow transplant." *Sedalia Democrat* (Sedalia, MO). 19 December 2009 <http://www.sedaliademocrat.com/articles/marrow-21021-draws-bone.html>.

[221] Source: Sophie Doughty, "Loving brother gives sister gift of life." *Evening Chronicle* (UK). 29 June 2007 <http://www.chroniclelive.co.uk/north-east-news/evening-chronicle-news/2007/06/29/loving-brother-gives-sister-gift-of-life-72703-19379214/>.

[222] Source: Sean McCann, compiler, *The Wit of Brendan Behan*, pp. 78, 111.

[223] Source: Alexander Woollcott, *Enchanted Aisles*, p. 91.

[224] Source: Harry "Steamboat" Johnson, *Standing the Gaff*, pp. 80-81.

[225] Source: Joe Garagiola, *It's Anybody's Ballgame*, pp. 32-33.

[226] Source: Ira L. Smith and H. Allen Smith, *Three Men on Third*, p. 190.

[227] Source: Tom Gorman and Jerome Holtzman, *Three and Two!*, p. 94.

[228] Source: John C. Skipper, *Umpires*, p. 118.

[229] Source: Ernestine Gichner Miller, *The Babe Book*, p. 100.

[230] Source: Algis Ruksenas, *Is That You Laughing Comrade?*, p. 142.

[231] Source: R. D. Wordsworth, compiler, *"Abe" Lincoln's Anecdotes and Stories*, p. 51.

[232] Source: Reggie Finlayson, *Colin Powell: People's Hero*, p. 32.

[233] Source: Chih Chung Tsai, *Zen Speaks*, pp. 42-43.

[234] Source: Patrick Barkham, "Nazis, needlework and my dad." *Guardian* (UK). 3 September 2011 <http://www.guardian.co.uk/lifeandstyle/2011/sep/03/tony-casdagli-father-stitching-nazis>.

[235] Source: Bob Dole, *Great Presidential Wit*, p. 35.

[236] Source: P. M. Zall, *George Washington Laughing*, pp. 25-26.

[237] Source: John Gielgud, *Distinguished Company*, p. 61.

[238] Source: Hiley H. Ward, editor, *Ecumania*, p. 123.

[239] Source: Sean McCann, compiler, *The Wit of Oscar Wilde*, p. 80.

[240] Source: Keith Elliot Greenberg, *Pro Wrestling: From Carnivals to Cable TV*, p. 32-34.

[241] Source: Jocko Conlan and Robert W. Creamer, *Jocko*, p. 143.

[242] Source: Jayne Torvill and Christopher Dean, *Torvill and Dean*, p. 176.

[243] Source: Mary Lou Retton and Bela Karolyi, *Mary Lou: Creating an Olympic Champion*, pp. 63-64.

[244] Source: Dick Hymen, *Potomac Wind and Wisdom*, p. 59.

[245] Source: Megan Howard, *Madeleine Albright*, p. 96.

[246] Source: Christina Lessa, *Gymnastics Balancing Acts*, p. 6

[247] Source: Richard Mackenzie, *A Wee Nip at the 19th Hole*, p. 84.

[248] Source: Mary Lou Retton and Bela Karolyi, *Mary Lou: Creating an Olympic Champion*, p. 83.

[249] Source: Claudia Miller, *Shannon Miller: My Child, My Hero*, p. 34.

[250] Source: Michael J. Pellowski, *Baseball's Funniest People*, p. 75.

www.ingramcontent.com/pod-product-compliance
Lightning Source LLC
Chambersburg PA
CBHW031349160726
47993CB00002B/883